C000220593

ST CUTHBERT OF
DURHAM

Philip Nixon

AMBERLEY

ACKNOWLEDGEMENTS

With thanks to St Laurence Church, Pittington, Durham; St Mary and St Cuthbert's Church, Chester-le-Street, Durham; Revd Canon Bryan Rowe, Rector of St Michael's Church, Workington, Cumbria. Also to Eric Frisby, Alan Brown, David Westall of Haydon Bridge, Val Nixon, Mark Nixon, Sophy Nixon, Archie the Labrador, and all the special people who gave me information and stories while I was taking photographs for this project.

And a special thanks to The Very Reverend Michael Sadgrove, Dean of Durham, and Lilian Groves MBE, Senior Guide for Durham Cathedral, for their unending kindness and patience. And also thanks to Nicola Gale of Amberley for being a truly excellent project manager.

First published 2012

Amberley Publishing
The Hill, Stroud
Gloucestershire, GL5 4EP

www.amberleybooks.com

British Library Cataloguing in Publication Data.
A catalogue record for this book is available from the British Library.

ISBN 978 1 4456 0361 2

Typeset in 10pt on 12pt Sabon.
Typesetting and Origination by Amberley Publishing.
Printed in the UK.

CONTENTS

Jarrow became the centre of Anglo-Saxon learning in the North of England, and was home to the Venerable Bede, who became the greatest and most respected Anglo-Saxon scholar.

INTRODUCTION

The story of St Cuthbert captured my imagination from an early age. To me it seemed not only wonderful but almost incredible that this remarkable man should be buried in the cathedral in my home city. I was filled with awe at the stories we were told at Junior School of St Cuthbert's life and the tale of his eventual arrival at Durham. End-of-term was a time of great excitement – we were shown around the magnificent cathedral and asked to bring 3d to school so we could go into the monk's dormitory. What an experience to see where the monks had slept – an even greater thrill was to be led into the dim, dark undercroft to see the skeleton of a whale ... creepy! I don't think anybody asked how it got there and certainly nobody made the association with the Prince Bishop's right of wreck and forfeiture. St Cuthbert is said to watch over the people of Durham and I feel that he has continued to inspire me personally on a professional level – one of the first long-term projects I took on, many years ago, when I took to photography full time, was a slide-tape programme on St Cuthbert. Since then I have wanted to write and illustrate his life story, to share as a celebration and enjoyment of his beginning, influence and legacy in the North. Indeed, the contemporary photographs in this book were taken especially for the project; they illustrate the sites of his visits both before and after his death. There are even some that have been influenced by his great cult following, hopefully to add another dimension of understanding to the story of this great saint. They say familiarity breeds contempt but it's just not true of St Cuthbert. The magnificent building that houses his shrine is still the epicentre of religion in the North and Cuthbert is still the beacon within that shrine – almost three quarters of a million visitors a year can't be wrong!

I haven't quoted many sources directly, apart from the Venerable Bede, because a lot of the information was kindly offered by individual vicars, churchwardens, lay preachers, and general enthusiasts as I travelled around taking photographs – it's amazing how many different views and ideas you get on the same subject by talking to different people! It's then a question of sifting and verifying information, as far as possible, from sources such as cathedral publications, the wonderful translation of the *Two Lives of St Cuthbert* by Bertram Colgrave, plus Stranks, Consitt, Marner and several other knowledgeable authors.

St Cuthbert has had a tremendous influence on the North – although there is nothing remaining of the sites directly connected with his time on Earth, his cult following was so huge that in many of the places he visited and indeed in many of the places where his body rested on its epic journey from Lindisfarne to Durham, churches have been founded and the secret and holy places are still there, allowing us to trace his remarkable life and follow his legacy. In his lifetime Cuthbert was an influential churchman. After his death, his grave in Lindisfarne, and the places to which his coffin was subsequently moved, became the greatest focus of pilgrimage in early medieval England. Durham Cathedral, one of the most magnificent cathedrals in the world, stands sentinel over his bones, and the tomb of this humble pioneer of Christianity in the North continues to be a place of pilgrimage.

Two life stories of St Cuthbert were written. The earlier biography was written in about AD 700–705 by an anonymous monk from Lindisfarne, and although there is great speculation as to his identity, it still remains an unsolved mystery. However, it is due to the endeavour of another great northern man, the Venerable Bede, that we have an accurate record of the saint's life. Bede described himself as 'a Servant of Christ and Priest of the Monastery of Saints Peter and Paul which is at Wearmouth and Jarrow'. We probably know him best as the author of the epic work, which he completed in AD 731, *The Ecclesiastical History of the English People*. This work is still in print – translated, of course – and it remains our primary source for understanding the beginnings of the English people and the coming of Christianity. Significantly, it is the first work of history to calculate dates from the birth of Christ. Bede's reputation during his own lifetime and indeed the few centuries after was founded on his commentaries on the books of the Bible, copies of which were found in the great monastic libraries all over Western Europe.

Bede was born in AD 673, possibly in the area covered by what is now Sunderland. We know nothing of his family background, except perhaps that his parents were quite wealthy because he was entrusted at the age of seven to the care of Benedict Biscop in the monastery of Wearmouth at Sunderland, near Durham. In AD 685, Bede moved with his second teacher Ceolfrid (to whom he was devoted) to the newly founded monastery at Jarrow. Records show that Bede spent the rest of his life in the monastery and only left to make visits to Lindisfarne and York and occasionally call on friends. He was ordained a deacon at the age of nineteen and a priest at thirty. He observed the rules of the monastery and was extremely conscientious in his attendance of choir at the daily offices. He also worked diligently as a scholar and teacher; and is recorded as saying, 'It has always been my delight to learn or to teach or to write. I have made it my business, for my own benefit, and that of my brothers, to make brief extracts from the works of the venerable fathers on the Holy Scriptures, or to add my own notes to make a clear interpretation of their meaning.'

The range of Bede's scholastic ability was nothing short of astonishing, going far beyond the writing of his *Ecclesiastical History*. Bishop Boniface, who led a mission to Germany, wrote of Bede that he 'shone forth as a lantern in the church by his scriptural commentary'. He wrote also of nature. He knew that the earth was a sphere. He had a sense of latitude and observed the annual movement of the sun into the north and south hemispheres from the evidence of varying lengths of shadows. He knew that the moon influenced the cycle of the tides. He wrote on calculating time and his exposition of the Great Cycle of 532 years was of fundamental value to the Church in the task of calculating the date of Easter. He wrote textbooks for his students on the theory and practice of ecclesiastical music – the earliest records of the Gregorian tradition in Britain.

Bede also wrote *The Life of St Cuthbert, Bishop of Lindisfarne* and although some historians regard it as uncritical and claim that it relates rather a large number of miracles taken as fact, Bede was inclined to rationalise and explore his statements; he was also able to interview a number of people who had personally known Cuthbert. He was, however, particularly scrupulous about recording the sources and authenticity of his information, and asked those who copied and edited his work to do likewise. Bede died in his cell at the monastery in 735. Cuthbert, a young monk who was with him, later wrote an account of his death. He describes how Bede continued to work and pray right up to the end and finished dictating a translation of the Gospel of St John. Then, knowing he was about to die, he said, 'I have a few treasures in my box, some pepper, a napkin ring and incense. Run quickly and fetch the priests of our monastery, and I will share among them such little presents as God has given me.' Bede was very highly regarded and beloved by his community and exceptionally well thought of by his contemporaries. He was buried at Jarrow, although around 1020 his body was removed from Jarrow and taken to Durham Cathedral by the sacrist Alfred Westoe, where it was first placed in a small linen bag in the same tomb as St Cuthbert. It was Bishop Pudsey who gave Bede his own shrine in 1370, described as a 'costly and magnificent shrine with a silver caskett gilt with gold'. This shrine was damaged in the Reformation, but the bones were reburied beneath the floor of the Galilee Chapel when the present tomb was erected in 1542.

The title Venerable began to be used within a couple of generations of his death as the high regard and influence of his writings became more widely known. The title was used by the influential Council of Aachen in 835 and this reference was referred to by Cardinal Wiseman and his English bishops when they approached the Holy See for Bede to be made a Doctor of the Church. However, it was not until 13 November 1899 that Pope Leo XIII decreed that the feast of the Venerable Bede be celebrated annually on 27 May – although it is now moved to the 25th. His influence was immense and may well have been greater still if the Vikings hadn't sacked the northern monasteries in the ninth century and probably destroyed some of his works. In his day he was probably the greatest scholar in Britain and, quite possibly, the world.

There are many miracles recorded in St Cuthbert's life and it is up to the modern reader to come to terms with them. Part of the explanation probably lies in the mentality of the people he lived among – they accepted the presence and existence of the supernatural and eagerly believed any demonstration of its power. Cuthbert was accepted very early in his life as a man of exceptional holiness; miracles would have been expected of him, and of course would have been readily seen and believed. Cuthbert himself had unquestioning faith in the power of God and was always ready to see His divine intervention directly at work. When his life story was written down, his biographers – and those who translated their work – would have been quite sure they were recording the deeds of a great saint. Equally, they would be sure that what God had done for one of his servants he would do for another, and this possibly led them to insert some miracles attributed to previous saints into their work – not with the intent to deceive or mislead, but to explain and emphasise what they believed to be the honourable truth of the events. There is, however, a strong possibility that Cuthbert did possess the strange healing power that some remarkable people are blessed with, although it is probably safe to say that not all of them would be identified as saints. It would be easy to dismiss the more improbable of these reports as mere superstition but if they are studied more closely, with deeper understanding, they always reveal something about Cuthbert himself or the people he lived among.

1
IN THE BEGINNING

In the seventh century the area that was to become the kingdom of Northumbria was a wild, untamed land. Its pagan inhabitants worshipped gods as savage as themselves. Their religion was enigmatic, ruled by myth and magic, and shrouded in mysterious belief. The people were in awe of nature and its forces. There were large areas of wild ancient forest inhabited by dangerous and deadly creatures that were feared, revered and believed to wield terrible magic. The civilising influence of the Romans had long since vanished.

However, things were destined to change when Edwin became king of his native Deira and neighbouring Bernicia, to form the kingdom of Northumbria. Edwin's reign marks an interruption of the otherwise constant domination of Northumbria by the Bernicians, and has been seen as 'contrary to the prevailing tendency'. At this time Edwin was great friends with Eadbald of Kent. Edwin arranged to marry Eadbald's sister, Ethelburga. We are told in the writings of the Venerable Bede that Eadbald would only give his consent to the marriage if Edwin agreed to convert to Christianity, because a Christian princess should not marry a pagan. Conversion to Chrisitianity in Kent had started as a direct consequence of the marriage of Eadbald's father Ethelbehrt to his Frankish mother, Bertha, and he hoped the same would happen in Northumbria. Edwin said that Ethelburga would be allowed to worship how she wished and that he would certainly listen to Christian preachers and seriously consider converting to Christianity himself. This was good enough for Ethelburga and she agreed to the marriage, travelling north in 625 and bringing with her the newly consecrated Bishop Paulinus as her chaplain.

Bede describes Paulinus as 'a man tall of stature, a little stooping, with black hair and a thin face, a hooked and thin nose, his aspect both venerable and awe-inspiring'. He was born in Italy and was sent to Kent by Pope Gregory I in 601 as part of a group of missionary monks, sent to continue the conversion of the Anglo-Saxons to Christianity.

Edwin listened to the preaching of Paulinus for many months and finally, after impressive correct predictions about the birth of his daughter Eanflaed and a failed assassination attempt by a mob of west-Saxons, he consulted his advisors. Both predictions were attibuted to the zeal of Christian prayers. Coifi, the high priest of the pagan religion, advised adopting Christianity, since he said that the pagan religion had not proved satisfactory and the other elders and counsellors were of the same opinion. This is where the well-known analogy comes from – some historians bellieve it was delivered by Coifi himself, others by another enthusiastic advisor to the king:

In AD 548, a royal settlement developed on this unassuming field north of Wooler and would go on to provide a regional residence for some of the greatest kings and queens of the day: Ethelfrith, Edwin and Ethelburga, the saintly Oswald, and his younger brother, Oswi.

Bede, writing his *Ecclesiastical History of the English People*, recounts how, when Edwin (AD 617–33) and his queen, Ethelburga, were residing at 'Ad Gefrin', her Italian bishop, Paulinus, spent thirty-six days: 'Catechising and baptising; during which days, from morning to night, he did nothing else but instruct the crowds who flocked to him from every village and district in the teaching of Christ, and when instructed, he washed them in the water of absolution in the river Glen, nearby.'

The present life of man upon earth, O King, seems to me in comparison with that time which is unknown to us like the swift flight of a sparrow through a mead-hall where you sit at supper in winter, with your Ealdormen and thanes, while the fire blazes in the midst and the hall is warmed, but the wintry storms of rain or snow are raging abroad. The sparrow, flying in at one door and immediately out at another, whilst he is within, is safe from the wintry tempest, but after a short space of fair weather, he immediately vanishes out of your sight, passing from winter to winter again. So this life of man appears for a little while, but of what is to follow or what went before we know nothing at all. If, therefore, this new doctrine tells us something more certain, it seems justly to be followed in our kingdom.

King Edwin and his advisors were baptised during Easter of 627; many other conversions followed and we are told by Bede that Paulinus laboured at Ad Gefrin, the Royal Palace, from dawn until dusk for thirty-six days non-stop, baptising the willing Northumbrians in the nearby River Glen.

This golden time was not to last, however; six years later King Edwin was defeated and killed by the pagan hordes of Cadwallon of Wales and Penda of Mercia at the Battle of Hatfield Chase. Cadwallon was actually a Christian, although his set of beliefs was vastly different from that held by Edwin and Paulinus. Paulinus fled back to Kent, taking Queen Ethelburga and her children with him. Northumbria was again plunged into dark times.

When Edwin had first taken the throne of Northumbria from Ethelfrith, his two sons, Oswald and Oswi, had fled to take refuge with the Celtic monks on the Isle of Iona, just off the west coast of Scotland.

News reached the island that Edwin was dead and that Northumbria had again been divided in two, but even worse, Cadwallon had killed both of these new kings and was ruling Northumbria – as a mighty tyrant, in the words of Bede. Oswald immediately raised a small army and returned to Northumbria. In 635 his army faced the huge forces commanded by Cadwallon on a sloping table of land, just above Chollerford, not far from the Roman Wall. Just before the battle Oswald gave orders for a wooden cross to be erected in full view of his army. He and his followers knelt before it and prayed to God to help their endeavour.

After a monumental struggle, the massed forces of Cadwallon's army were defeated – they turned and fled, hotly pusued by Oswald's small force. Cadwallon himself was eventually caught and killed at a place that has been identified as Rowley Burn, near Hexham.

There is evidence to suggest that most of the conflict took place in a field called Mound's Close, to the south of the present road that bisects this ancient battlefield – a number of skulls and fragments of weapons have been uncovered during ploughing. The place where King Oswald, as he became known, raised the cross is said to have been the site of many miraculous cures. St Oswald's Church, set in glorious isolation on the northern edge of the battlefield, was built in 1737 to commemorate the battle. However, it was extensivley repaired and altered in 1887 and it was during these works that a large silver coin depicting St Oswald was found. On one side was a representation of Oswald's head, and on the obverse was a cross. This was used for a time by the monastery at Durham

The island of Iona, off the west coast of Scotland, is the symbolic centre of Scottish Christianity. Throughout its 1,400 years of history, its fortunes have fluctuated, from its peak as one of the greatest centres of learning in Dark Age Europe, to its nadir as a crumbling ruin left by Viking raiders.

as their common seal in his honour. The basic eighteenth-century rectangular shape of the church is still in evidence, together with an interesting dated sundial. Nineteenth-century alterations include the south porch and the unusual bell cote. Inside the church is a decorated Roman altar, which looks like it has been modified to serve as the socket for a cross – possibly the predecessor of the modern roadside cross seen today?

After the joyous and successful outcome of the Battle of Heavenfield, as it became known, Oswald lost no time in sending to Iona for missionaries to reconvert the Northumbrians to Christianity. We are told by the Venerable Bede that 'brother Corman and the first monks who came were beaten by the intractable nature of the people they had come to teach', and so went home. The next monk to try was the wise and gentle Aidan who, with the help of King Oswald, established a monastery and school at Lindisfarne, and from here he began his life's work of spreading the word of Christianity. The king and Aidan enjoyed a good partnership – Oswald sometimes having to interpret the words of Aidan, who was not fluent in the English language.

The monastery on Iona was hugely successful, and played a crucial role in the conversion to Christianity of the Picts of present-day Scotland in the late sixth century, and of the Anglo-Saxon kingdom of Northumbria in 635. It was from here that missionaries were summoned to reconvert the Northumbrians to Christianity after King Oswald's resounding victory at the Battle of Heavenfield.

After the death of Oswald in 642 while fighting Penda of Mercia at the Battle of Maserfield, Northumbria separated temporarily into its two constituent kingdoms of Bernicia and Deira. Oswald's brother Oswi became king in Bernicia, and Oswin became king in Deira. Bede describes Oswin as 'a man of handsome appearance and great stature, who was pleasant in his speech and courteous in his manner'. Aidan and Oswin became great friends and continued Oswald's good work together. Aidan not only taught people in church; he also went out into the villages and countryside of Northumbria to spread the word and, indeed, is said to have been so successful in his efforts that he once baptised 15,000 people in the space of a week.

Aidan was a dedicated missionary and would walk from one village to another engaging in gentle conversation with the people he met, slowly and quietly interesting them in Christianity.

Aidan lived a frugal life and he persuaded the laity to do likewise, encouraging them to fast and to study the scriptures. He himself fasted on Wednesdays and Fridays, and very rarely ate at the royal table; on those occasions when a feast was set before him, he would give the food away to the hungry.

One story tells of how the king gave Aidan a horse to make his travelling easier, but Aidan gave the horse to a beggar. Oswin was very angry until, as Bede explains, Aidan asked if the son of a mare was more precious to the king than a son of God. Oswin

Thanks to the fame of its monastic founder, St Columba, the island has always been revered as a holy place, and, over the centuries, has continued to be a place of pilgrimage.

apologised and sought Aidan's pardon, and promised never again to question or regret any of his wealth being given away to children of God.

By patiently talking to the people on their own level, Aidan and his monks slowly and gently introduced Christianity to the Northumbrians. Aidan also took twelve English boys into training at the monastery, to ensure that the area's future religious leadership would be English.

The monastery Aidan established grew and its monks helped found churches and other monasteries all over the North. It also became a centre of learning and a store of scholarly knowledge. In their first year at one of Aidan's monasteries the novices would learn all the psalms, in Latin, by heart; they would then move on to learning the Gospels, also in Latin, and also by heart.

The Venerable Bede would later write about Aidan and describe the many miracles attributed to him. One instance is described in which, in 651, a pagan army led by the dreaded Penda of Mercia attacked Bamburgh and tried to burn it down. Aidan prayed for the city, after which the winds turned and many of the besiegers were destroyed by fire.

In 651, Oswin was treacherously murdered at Gilling in North Yorkshire, on the orders of Oswi, who then became ruler of a reunited Northumbria. Twelve days later, on

Left: On the eve of the Battle of Heavenfield, Oswald ordered a wooden cross to be made and erected in full view of his army. He knelt with his followers and prayed to God to assist them in their task.

Below: Legend has it that, the night before the battle, a worried Oswald was visited by St Columba in a vision and told that he would be victorious. After a monumental struggle, the pagan forces were defeated, and Cadwallon was killed.

31 August, Aidan died, seventeen years after his arrival in Northumbria. He had fallen ill while at Bamburgh castle and died leaning against the buttress of the nearby church for support. There is now no trace of that wooden building, other than perhaps a beam over the font in the baptistery of the modern church – tradition has it that this is the only surviving relic of this first church. It serves no structural function and is believed to have supported the awning under which Aidan died. Mention of this beam is made by Bede who claims that this is the beam St Aidan was leaning against when he died; it is then said to have miraculously survived two fires. Aidan's death is marked by a simple shrine within the present church, which dates from the end of the twelfth century.

At the time of the Battle of Heavenfield, a boy was born in the Border Hills who was destined to become one of the greatest religious icons of the North – his name was Cuthbert.

Thy tower, proud Bamburgh, mark'd they there,
King Ida's castle, huge and square.

Above is how Sir Walter Scott described Bamburgh in his epic poem *Marmion*. However, he was guilty of a little over-enthusiasm, as the castle did not look like it does today until over 700 years after the reign of King Ida! It was King Ethelfrith the Destroyer, grandson of Ida the Flamebearer, who gave the fortress to his wife, Queen Bebba. She renamed it *Bebbanburgh*, from which the name Bamburgh is derived.

A place of worship was founded on the site of the present Bamburgh church in 635 by St Aidan, who was called to Bamburgh from Iona by King Oswald to re-establish Christianity in his newly reunited kingdom of Northumbria. There is now no trace of that wooden building – other than perhaps a beam over the font in the baptistery. Tradition has it that this is the only relic of the first church; it serves no structural function but Bede mentions that this is the beam St Aidan was leaning against when he died. It is said to have miraculously survived two fires.

The place of St Aidan's death is marked by a simple shrine within the present church, which dates from the end of the twelfth century.

2
CUTHBERT AS A BOY

Nothing much is known about Cuthbert's birth, but it is known that from about the age of eight he was brought up by a foster mother called Kenswiv. This leads us to believe that Cuthbert was born of noble parents; it was the custom at that time, in Northern England and Ireland, for boys of high birth to be traditionally given into the care of foster mothers to be raised to manhood. One story of his early boyhood survives, indeed told by Cuthbert himself to Bishop Trumwine – the only Bishop of Northumbria ever – who in turn related it to Bede:

> A group of children were playing traditional games of running, jumping and wrestling in a field somewhere in what is today the Scottish Borders. One particularly handsome young fellow outshone his friends in his ability to run faster and jump higher – and would defeat all challengers in the wrestling ring. When the others had collapsed, exhausted and worn out, he would be left standing like a victorious gladiator, waiting for, and encouraging, someone to challenge him. In the middle of all this frantic action a small child, about three years old ran up to him begging him in the most serious manner, 'to be steadfast and leave this foolish play'. His cries were ignored and the tiny child flung himself on to the ground in an overwhelming tantrum. Concerned, the older children asked him what was wrong and pointing at the handsome boy he exclaimed, 'Oh Cuthbert, most holy bishop and priest, it is not befitting your dignity, or that of your high office, to be showing off your agility and these unnatural tricks when the Lord has consecrated you to be a teacher of virtue to everyone, including your elders!' Cuthbert, being kind and generous, listened carefully to this astonishing tirade whilst soothing the distressed infant with kind attention. Carefully considering the implication of this prophecy Cuthbert abandoned his frivolous games and returned home, determined from that day to become more thoughtful and steadier in his disposition.

We can only guess that Cuthbert must have led the normal life for a lad in the seventh century because sadly our knowledge of the social conditions at that time is somewhat limited. Northumbria then covered the area from the River Humber to the Firth of Forth and there were large areas of forest only inhabited by wild animals, although there were villages of wood huts or wattle and daub dwellings scattered around the more open areas. Hadrian's Wall would have been a prominent feature, running from Wallsend to Carlisle, a reminder of the Roman Occupation – and Cuthbert must

Sheep are still grazed on the beautiful and tranquil Kyloe Hills, just as they were when a vision of St Aidan's body being taken to Heaven by a host of angels convinced a shepherd boy by the name of Cuthbert to follow a spiritual life and become a monk at the monastery of Melrose.

have been familiar with the many Roman buildings in such places as Chester-le-Street, Carlisle, Corbridge and South Shields. However, these remains don't seem to have inspired the Anglo-Saxons to build in grand style, and even the well-educated monks preferred to use either the existing ruins or to build small huts grouped around a central church, in the style of the Irish settlers. Agriculture flourished and there are references to ploughs drawn by oxen; however, many of the inhabitants were nomadic and sheep, cattle, pigs and goats were herded all over the unfenced countryside. It was usual for young lads, even those from wealthy families, to spend their early lives as herdsmen, guarding their stock, with the help of their dogs, from the attentions of the many wolves that roamed ancient Northumbria.

Merchants brought silks, gold, precious stones, wine, oils, copper, tin and brass from overseas. Nobles owned many slaves – one of Aidan's earliest tasks had been the freeing of slaves, whom he then trained to serve the church. Monasteries and nunneries were established all over Northumbria thanks to Aidan's enthusiasm and zeal – there were no other centres of culture and learning – and these religious communities provided excellent schools with immense influence. And so it was in these changing times that Cuthbert grew up.

There are only a few recorded miracles of Cuthbert's boyhood and the first concerns the healing of a swollen knee. He had been suffering with this affliction for some time and could barely walk. One day he had been carried out of the house by servants and was lying on a small bed in the open air when a horseman of noble appearance, dressed entirely in white, appeared riding a strikingly fine animal. He asked if Cuthbert could help him with refreshment and tend to his horse. Cuthbert said he would be happy to do so if it were not for his badly inflamed knee. The rider dismounted. He examined the knee and said, 'Boil some wheat flour in milk and apply this hot poultice to your knee and it will be healed.' The rider remounted and rode away. Cuthbert followed the advice and was, indeed, healed in a few days. Of this Bede says, 'If anyone finds it difficult to believe that Cuthbert was visited by an angel on horseback they should consult the history of the Maccabees in which angels on horseback are said to have appeared to defend Judas Maccabaeus and the Temple itself.'

We are told by Bede that henceforth Cuthbert further devoted himself to God and, as he explained to his friends, when he prayed for help in pressing difficulties, he often found angels were sent to help him. He said that God listened to him because he in turn often devoted himself to praying for those in equally difficult circumstances. An occasion that illustrates his thoughtfulness and of prayers for others being answered is related by Bede about an incident that occurred at the mouth of the River Tyne. In Cuthbert's day there was a monastery here and the monks would bring wood by raft from upriver; one day a group of monks were guiding their rafts into the riverbank and a sudden gale rose from the west, scattered the rafts and drove them towards the mouth of the river – the monks from the monastery tried to help but the wind was much too strong and defeated their efforts. Realising that human aid was beyond them, the monks on the shore called on the divine and while the rafts were floating out to sea they gathered on the headland and prayed fervently to the Lord to save their brethren, who looked like they may perish at any minute. The answer to their prayers was long delayed but Cuthbert was standing on the opposite bank among a large crowd of peasants watching the incident – while the monks watched the rafts being washed away the peasants began to jeer at their misfortune – mocking the monks for their way of life, saying they deserved such misfortune for spurning the life of ordinary men and introducing new and strange rules of behaviour. Cuthbert admonished the peasants and told them to be more sympathetic and pray for the monks' safety rather than gloat over their misfortune. However the peasants were determined and argued against Cuthbert's plea saying that nobody would pray for these monks and God wouldn't help them, that they deserved their misfortune because they had done away with the old pagan ways, breeding confusion, and now nobody knew what to do. It had been only about fifteen years since King Oswald had brought Aidan from Iona to re-establish Christianity in Northumbria and paganism still struggled for supremacy. Cuthbert listened to their argument and then knelt down and, prostrating himself, prayed. At once the wind eased and changed direction, bringing the monks safely into land at a convenient place near to their monastery. The peasants were contrite and very ashamed of their behaviour. They gave due credit to Cuthbert's faith and from that moment on offered continual praise to God. Bede was told this story by one of the brethren of the monastery who claimed he had heard the tale from one of the peasants as he told a large group about the miracle.

On another occasion, Cuthbert was riding north and, after a long day's journey, crossed the River Wear at Chester-le-Street. Worried about food for his horse he arrived at a lonely farm. The woman of the house offered him the opportunity to rest a while and said she would provide food for him and his horse – he turned down the offer of a meal for himself since it was Friday and a day of fasting. The woman warned him that there were no other farms within a day's journey, but still Cuthbert insisted on continuing his fast. He continued his journey and indeed the advice had been correct, there were no other farms or homesteads to be seen. Fortunately he saw a deserted old shepherd's hut, or *sheiling*, that had been constructed for temporary accommodation over the summer. He went inside, intending to stay the night. He tethered his horse and gave it an armful of straw he had collected from bits that had been blown out of the roof. He settled down to prayer and contemplation but upon looking up he saw his horse lift its head and start pulling straw from the roof – suddenly a linen cloth fell with the straw. After his prayers he went to investigate and found to his delight a still warm, small loaf of bread and a portion of meat, enough for one meal, wrapped in the cloth. Cuthbert said, 'Oh God I was fasting for the love of thee and in return thou hast fed me and my animal. Blessed be Thy Name.' Cuthbert broke the bread and gave half to his horse and from that day on, he says, he was much more ready to fast after being fed by the Lord in his need and solitude.

Cuthbert had no sudden great revelation or call to the monastic life but all his life he seems to have moved with lovable ease and grace, which never left him, nearer and nearer to the devout way. It was, however, a Heavenly vision that finally caused him to abandon his secular life for that of a monk – but the vision was not a crisis – it was more a culmination of the many signs that God had already given to indicate that he was to live a life of dedication to His service. One night Cuthbert, together with a group of other young shepherds, was tending flocks in the Border Hills. While Cuthbert watched and prayed his companions slept. A shaft of bright light suddenly streamed from the sky and through it a Heavenly host descended to earth and, taking with them a shining bright soul, returned to Heaven. Cuthbert was deeply moved – he woke his companions and told them about his vision. The following morning he heard that Aidan, the much-loved Bishop of Lindisfarne, had died at Bamburgh at the very time he had seen the Heavenly host. Cuthbert returned the sheep he was tending to their owners and set out directly for the monastery at Melrose.

3

CUTHBERT THE MONK

Cuthbert chose to become a monk at Melrose because of the stories he had heard of its prior, Boisil. The monastery at Old Melrose was burned down by Kenneth MacAlpin in 839, but was originally sited on a small hill in a loop of the river about 2½ miles to the east of the existing priory ruins. Bede describes the scene in detail – Prior Boisil, together with a young monk called Sigfrith and one or two others, was standing at the gates of the monastery when they saw a young man on horseback and his servant approaching. They stopped at the monastery and the rider dismounted and passed the reins of his horse and the spear he was carrying to his servant. The monks noticed he was a particularly fine young man of pleasing appearance as he went into the church to pray. It is not known for certain that Boisil had any previous knowledge of Cuthbert and his intention to become a monk, but at the sight of him a vision came to the saintly prior and he instantly knew how great this young man was going to be in his later life. He exclaimed to his companions, 'Behold! The servant of the Lord!' This statement obviously had a very profound effect on the young Sigfrith because he repeated it, along with the incident, many years later to Bede in his monastery at Jarrow.

Boisil welcomed Cuthbert to Melrose with joy and kindness and after a few days, when Eata, the abbot, returned from his pastoral visits, the prior obtained permission for Cuthbert to receive the tonsure and join the brethren. Cuthbert soon settled into the daily routine of the monastery and became even more diligent than the others in reading and working, and watching and praying. He abstained from all intoxicants and fasted just sufficiently to still maintain his fit young body for the hard manual labour in which he so delighted. However, throughout his life he did subject his body to continual mortification, such as going whole nights without sleep and praying while standing up to his neck in water. However, these spectacular forms of asceticism – practised by the Irish monks and their followers from the fifth century onward – had gradually disappeared by the seventh century with the introduction of the rule of St Benedict into the Northumbrian monasteries; the hard life of obedience to this common rule was considered enough encouragement to attain sanctification.

Cuthbert had lived under Boisil's guidance for six or seven years when he was transferred, with some of his brethren, to a new monastery at Ripon. King Alchfrith gave the site at Ripon to the abbot Eata, who built the monastery and ruled over the community. Cuthbert was still in his early twenties but was appointed Guestmaster, an office of considerable importance. Religious communities placed hospitality among their greatest virtues and no brother would be appointed to this position unless he possessed great tact and virtue – Bede tells us that Cuthbert was both affable and pleasant in manner – valuable qualities for a brother who was to be the contact with the outside world for the monastery.

A story concerning a Heavenly traveller presents an insight not only to the zeal of the young Guestmaster but also a glimpse of the day-to-day monastery life. Early one snowy winter's morning, Cuthbert went to the guest chamber and discovered a young man inside, starved with hunger and cold. Cuthbert took pity on the traveller and immediately washed his numbed hands and feet, drying them vigorously with a warm towel to restore the circulation. The visitor stood as if to leave but Cuthbert asked him to stay a short while longer, until about 9.00 a.m., when a meal could be served. The brethren only took one meal during the day, at about 3.00 p.m. but visitors and travellers were allowed to break their fast much earlier. There was not much to lay before the guest – a few scraps from the previous day – but Cuthbert set a table and asked the visitor to begin the frugal meal while he went to the kitchen for some of the new bread which was being baked. However, the bread was not ready and Cuthbert returned without it to the guest chamber – but the visitor had vanished – he had gone without even leaving any footprints in the newly fallen snow.

Melrose Abbey was founded in 1136 by King David I and, because it was so close to the border, often suffered attacks by English armies. In 1322, Edward II desecrated and burned the abbey – it was rebuilt with help from Robert the Bruce, only to be destroyed again in 1385 by Richard II. The sacrilege was inevitably repeated by the Earl of Hertford in 1545 – it seems that English monarchs and their nobility took a perverse delight in destroying the sacred edifices of Scotland – and did so with unrestrained vigour.

St Cuthbert joined the monastery at Old Melrose, which was sited about 2 miles away from the present abbey on a relatively isolated peninsula, regarded by the monks as a place of peace and spiritual closeness to God. This site is recognised as one of the original and most important holy sites in Scotland and Northern England.

Above left: The crypt in Ripon Cathedral incorporates stone that was probably salvaged from nearby Roman ruins, and reveals building methods that were largely unknown in England at the time. To this day, visitors still come from near and far, as they have done since the seventh century, to offer prayers in Wilfrid's crypt.

Above right: Wilfrid was one of the most influential – and one of the most controversial – figures in the early English church. He was born into an aristocratic Northumbrian family in 634, and joined the monastery on Lindisfarne as a teenager, before making the first of his three trips to Rome. On his way back to England, he spent three years with the Bishop of Lyons, where he became a great follower of the ways of the continental church.

Completely mystified, Cuthbert carried the table back to the store house and as he entered he was met with the warm fragrant odour of newly baked bread. There were three excellent loaves of exceptional whiteness in front of him. Trembling, Cuthbert fell to his knees and said to himself, 'I can see that this was an angel of the Lord that I received and that he came to feed and not be fed.'

Cuthbert related this story to his brethren, but it is rare that he tells stories of miracles that concern himself, and Bede seems concerned that Cuthbert may seem boastful and firmly explains how seldom this happened. He says that if at all possible on these occasions, Cuthbert would tell the story with great humility in veiled terms – as if it had happened to someone else – emphasising his uncommon virtue and complete lack of vanity.

Eata and his brethren had only lived at Ripon for about three years when they were expelled for refusing to accept the Roman Church's date for keeping Easter, among other differences. Northumbria had been originally converted to Christianity through the teachings of Paulinus, who came north from the Roman mission in Kent in 625. This was short-lived and after the death of King Edwin the region reverted to paganism; but with the arrival of Aidan from Iona, after the Battle of Heavenfield, it was reconverted to the Celtic ways of Christianity. And so, in Cuthbert's youth, both the Roman and the Celtic ways were to be found in Northumbria. The Celtic and the Roman followers began to find themselves at variance over many things – the service to be used in baptism, and the shape of the tonsure. The Irish Church was firmly based on Biblical teaching and was monastically based while the Roman Church was more urban-based. But further, deeper differences began to appear, such as when it was appropriate to celebrate Easter. When the king ended his time of fasting and celebrated Easter, the queen and her followers were still fasting and celebrating Palm Sunday; the king and queen were celebrating Easter at different times. In fact, things got so complicated that Easter was celebrated twice in one year. The whole argument came to a head in 664 at the Synod of Whitby, when Northumbria finally decided in favour of the Roman Church. King Alchfrith, patron of the Ripon monastery, had already been greatly influenced by the up-and-coming ecclesiastic, Wilfrid, who had recently returned from Rome and was full of overwhelming enthusiasm for its customs. Alchfrith forthwith issued an ultimatum to the community at Ripon to either accept the Roman ways, or depart. The monks returned to Melrose where the Celtic customs predominated.

Only a few months after Cuthbert's return to Melrose, a severe epidemic of the plague ravaged the monastery. Epidemics of the plague were common in the seventh century and varied in their severity, but this was a devastating outbreak and spread throughout the whole of England. Boisil and Cuthbert were both stricken seriously ill with the disease. Cuthbert was so ill that the brethren spent a whole night in devout prayer for him. At dawn one of the monks told him what they had done. Cuthbert exclaimed, 'Then why am I lying here! Surely God has not refused to listen to the prayers of so many good men! Bring me my staff and sandals!' He immediately got out of his bed and tried to walk, leaning on his staff. He found his strength returning gradually until he was cured, except for a swelling which had developed on his thigh and which was to give him chronic pain for the rest of his life.

Wilfrid returned to Northumbria in 658 and was appointed abbot of the newly founded monastery at Ripon. He immediately ordered the building of a new stone church on the site where the present cathedral stands. He brought craftsmen from the Continent to build the new church dedicated to St Peter in 672. The only part of Wilfrid's original church is the ancient Saxon crypt; possibly making it the oldest church building in England to have remained in continuous use. St Wilfrid also introduced the Benedictine Rule for his monks, along with the most up-to-date Roman customs.

York's first Minster was built for the baptism of the Anglo-Saxon king Edwin of Northumbria. Edwin was christened in a small wooden church that had been built for the occasion, within the site of the first Roman fort. This event took place on Easter Sunday in 627. Soon after, Edwin ordered that this small wooden church should be rebuilt in stone.

Above left: It is interesting to note that, in the early 1440s, the soaring St Cuthbert window was added to York Minster, depicting events in his life, and, indeed, serves to illustrate the powerful influence the cult of St Cuthbert was having in the North.

Above right: York Minster survived the Viking age but was badly damaged by fire in 1069 when the Normans took control during the Harrying of the North. In 1080 Thomas of Bayeux became Archbishop and started the construction of a new cathedral that grew into the Minster of today. His vast Norman church was completed around 1100, and the base of some of its distinctive columns can still be seen in the crypt.

Cuthbert's strength soon returned and he went to visit his beloved friend, Prior Boisil, who was not surprised to see his excellent recovery, saying:

See brother, you've recovered from the affliction that troubled you, and I can definitely say that you will not die. However, it is I who am about to die and I would advise you to learn from me quickly because I have only seven days of health and strength left in which to teach you.

Cuthbert was deeply moved by these words but didn't doubt the accuracy of Boisil's prophecy for one moment. He asked, 'Which book would it be best to read if we only have a week?'

'The Evangelist John,' replied the prior. 'I have a copy which has seven chapters, one of which we can get through every day, reading and discussing it between ourselves as necessary.'

This they did and were able to finish the Gospel because, as Bede says, 'They dealt with only the simple things of the faith which worketh by love and not deep matters of argument.'

It was possibly through watching the brave old man's lack of concern over his death that Cuthbert learned that faith and love were more important than any matters of dispute. This was probably why, at a time of growing dissent and dispute over religious matters, Cuthbert never became involved in any arguments nor got involved in any great contentions, but calmly held on to his principles in the face of such difficulty, perhaps best illustrated by his coming time on Lindisfarne.

Boisil and Cuthbert had long, intimate talks during the few remaining days of the prior's life and he was able to foretell Cuthbert's future life to him, including the prophecy that he would be made a bishop. However, Cuthbert told no one of this although it must have reminded him of the incident when he was a young boy and a child addressed him as 'holy bishop and priest' in front of his friends.

After Boisil's death Cuthbert was appointed Prior of Melrose and both through teaching and example he demonstrated how the rule should be obeyed. Continuing

Whitby Abbey
During the seventh century, Christianity in Britain existed in two forms of differing liturgical practices, generally referred to as the Celtic and Roman traditions. The Celtic practice was that of the Irish monks who lived in the monastery on the isle of Iona, whereas the Roman tradition kept observances according to the customs of Rome. Consequently, the Synod of Whitby was summoned in 664 at St Hilda's double monastery to decide the future of Christian teaching and worship.

Cuddy's Cave, Dod Law
Cuddy's Cave can be found on the southern slope of Dod Law, near Wooler. It is traditionally associated with St Cuthbert and the itinerant preaching of his early days.

Teviot Valley
Cuthbert and a young assistant were on a missionary journey in the wild valley of the River Teviot when an eagle provided their next meal.

the work of his predecessor, he spent a lot of time travelling great distances to teach the Gospel. Sometimes he went on horseback but more often on foot; he was usually away for around a week but sometimes as long as a month. There was a lot of work to do because during the plague epidemic there had been a desperate backsliding into heathenism. The terrified peasants had forgotten their baptisms and turned instead to the use of incantations, amulets and other 'mysteries of devilish art' – Bede says, almost mockingly, as if these pagan beliefs would have been of any help. It took all the power of Cuthbert's zeal and warmth of character to persuade these terrified people back to the true faith. His devotion to preaching drove him specially to seek out those villages and settlements situated in remote and dangerous places that others feared to visit, and to convert those poor and ignorant people that other teachers were unable to reach.

Cuthbert's influence went from strength to strength with his associated signs and miracles. On one occasion he and two brethren had set sail for the land of the Picts, just after Christmas. Shortly after their arrival they were unable to start their journey because of a fierce storm and they began to suffer from extremely distressing cold and desperate hunger. However, when the day of the Epiphany arrived Cuthbert offered comfort to his companions by gently suggesting that they pray to God to feed them. He then led them to the sea shore and they found three portions of dolphin flesh, freshly prepared for cooking; the little party of monks fell to their knees and gave thanks to God.

At another time Cuthbert, accompanied by a young monk, was travelling along the banks of the River Teviot on one of his missionary journeys when, as they walked, the young boy asked, 'Where will we partake of our mid-day meal?' The prior answered, 'My son, you may rest assured that the Lord will provide food for those who trust him.' Looking up, Cuthbert pointed out an eagle quartering the sky above the river and said, 'If he so pleased, the Lord could provide us with food with the help of that bird.' As they walked they saw the eagle land on the riverbank and Cuthbert told the boy to go and see what food she had brought from the Lord. The young monk came back with a large fish that the eagle had just taken from the river, but Cuthbert asked, 'What have you done my son? You should have given our provider her share – quickly, cut it in half and take her a fair portion for her labours.' The boy followed his instructions and Cuthbert took the other half of the fish and asked a family in the next dwelling they came upon to cook it. They shared a satisfying meal together before Cuthbert and his companion continued their journey.

Cuthbert's fame rapidly spread all over Northumbria. He received an invitation from the abbess Ebba to visit her community at Coldingham, near Berwick. The monastery here was a double, with monks and nuns living in the same place but in different dwellings. It was controlled by the abbess Ebba, the sister of King Oswi and King Oswald. It was the tradition in those days that a woman of noble birth should hold such an important position. And, in fact, Hilda, who presided over one of the most famous double monasteries at Whitby, was the great niece of King Edwin.

Surprisingly no scandal was associated with these institutions in those days, with the exception of Coldingham, which – according to Bede's account – was consumed by fire in punishment for the wickedness and corruption that took place here; we can only guess at the depravity that was rife here, but it was at a time when Ebba was old and infirm and unable enforce the strict rules. However, in the account of Cuthbert's visit to Coldingham, no unseemliness is mentioned in connection with the monastery.

Cuthbert's attitude to women was always friendly – he had many women friends he often visited and in all probability the legendary dislike of women which was later attributed to him was nothing more than a vicious rumour started by the Normans who, at a time when there was a belief in the inferiority and impurity of women, found it beneficial to attribute this fashionable prejudice to him. The truth is that in Anglo-Saxon England women were highly regarded and the fact that they were often appointed to rule over double monasteries proved that they were greatly respected for their intelligence, organisational ability and piety.

Ebba's monastery at Coldingham was built on a high, windswept cliff now known as St Abb's Head, with magnificent commanding views of the surrounding sea and landscape.

During his stay, Cuthbert would sneak out alone every night down to the sea shore to watch and pray and secretly return in the morning to join the brethren in worship. But one night one of the brethren saw him leave and, keen to know what he was doing, followed him down the precipitous winding path. This monk saw Cuthbert enter the water up to his armpits in the sea swell. Watching furtively from behind a rocky

St Abb's Head
Among the places visited by Cuthbert during his lifetime was the Monastery of Coldingham. This famous monastery was one of those founded by St Aidan and afterwards became a cell to the great Benedictine monastery at Durham. It was built upon a high rock overlooking the sea, a short distance to the south of St Abb's Head, which takes its name from St Ebba, its first abbess.

outcrop he could see Cuthbert praying and occasionally hear his voice singing praises over the sound of the breaking waves. Cuthbert left the water at daybreak and made his way on to the small rocky beach. Immediately two little animals came up on to the shore and lay down beside him; they licked his feet and rolled against them, wiping them with their fur and drying them with their breath. Cuthbert gave the animals a blessing and they returned to the sea. Bede refers to these animals as sea otters but in all probability they were two of the grey seals that are common in the North Sea off the Northumbrian coast. Cuthbert hurried back to the monastery but the monk who secretly watched him was so overcome with what he had witnessed that he hid himself among the rocks, terrified and trembling. It wasn't until much later in the morning he was able to make his way back to the monastery. At once he prostrated himself in front of Cuthbert and begged forgiveness because he never doubted that the prior had known what he had done. Cuthbert granted his pardon but said that he must tell no one what he had seen until after his death. The penitent monk kept his promise but told many what he had witnessed after Cuthbert had died.

Coldingham Beach

Cuthbert's routine was to spend a part of the night in prayer, and for this purpose he left the monastery when the brethren were asleep. A monk secretly followed Cuthbert and saw him walk down to the beach and wade into the sea until the water reached his neck. He spent most of the night singing praises to God. At dawn he came out of the water, fell to his knees, and concluded his prayers. A local tradition still lingers amongst the people of the coast that two otters came out from the rocks, warmed his half-frozen feet by licking them and drying them with their fur. When they had finished Cuthbert blessed them and dismissed them. He returned to the monastery to join with the monks chanting matins. To the watching monk this had seemed like a miracle, and he was so overcome with remorse, thinking he had sinned by spying, that he confessed to Cuthbert, who instantly forgave him but asked that he should not tell anyone until after his death. After Cuthbert died, the monk told many of the miracle he had witnessed.

4
CUTHBERT AS PRIOR

Eata, who was abbot of both Melrose and Lindisfarne, transferred Cuthbert to the monastery on Lindisfarne as prior when he was about thirty years old. On his arrival he found the brethren somewhat lacking in discipline. He patiently discussed with them the traditions that were to be introduced now that the king had accepted the Roman way of worship. During these meetings, the new prior's introductions were debated with heat and anger. Bede tells us how Cuthbert dealt with this disappointing response:

> When he was wearied by the sharp contentions of his opponents he would rise up suddenly and with placid appearance and demeanour he would depart, thus dissolving the Chapter, but nevertheless on the following day, as if he had suffered no opposition the day before, he would give the same exhortations again to the same company until he gradually converted them to his own views.

Cuthbert's strength, patience and spirituality commanded a great and increasing respect from the monks. The asceticism that he demonstrated by spending three or four nights without sleep while he indulged in hard manual labour or walked around the island, keeping himself awake by singing psalms, further endeared him to the brethren. Throughout all this Cuthbert's happy and lovable nature and personal penitence were easy companions to his hard outward discipline which turned their great respect into a deep and lasting affection for him. He was so full of genuine compassion that when anyone was confessing their sins to him he would often be the first to show tears of emotion out of pity for their weakness.

Lindisfarne, or Holy Island as it is also known, is a tidal island and at low tide a narrow causeway connects it with the mainland – this allowed Cuthbert to continue his work visiting people on the mainland as well as ruling over the members of the religious community on the island – he rapidly became as famous as he had been at Melrose for his teaching, preaching and miracles.

We are told that while on his journeys in the western districts of Berwickshire, he often visited Kenswiv, the devout woman who had been his nurse from the first years of his boyhood. On one occasion, while he was preaching to the people of the village where she lived – possibly Wrangholm, which lies between the Leader and the Tweed – a fire broke out and raged violently, its flames fanned by a high wind, endangering his foster-mother's house and all those around it.

Above left: St Aidan and his twelve monks lived a life of prayer, study and austerity on Lindisfarne and set about converting the northern Anglo-Saxons from paganism to Christianity.

Above right: St Mary's Church, Lindisfarne, stands on the site of the wooden church built by St Aidan. This was replaced by a small stone church in Anglo-Saxon times, but it was the Benedictine Monks of Durham who, while building the second monastery, decided St Mary's should be the parish church of Lindisfarne.

Lindisfarne Priory
The remains visible today are those of the twelfth-century priory established by monks from Durham Cathedral. The decorated piers are copied from those at Durham.

Cuthbert saw the imminent danger to those he loved and threw himself face down on the ground praying fervently – the wind suddenly changed, and the flames were immediately quenched and disaster prevented.

Cuthbert worked hard among the monks and villagers but for many years he had looked forward to a different way of life – he had served the community for twelve years as prior when, in the words of Bede, 'He was now held worthy to rise to the repose of divine contemplation'; in other words, he was to become a hermit.

His withdrawal was gradual; at first he retired to a small rocky island about one hundred and fifty metres south-west of the priory – it is surrounded by water at high tide but can be reached by a rough ridge of very slippery stones at low tide. The ruins of an ancient chapel and a large poignant cross mark this place, now known as St Cuthbert's Isle, and although he remained here for a while he still sought a place of retreat further and more remote from mankind.

The place he chose was Inner Farne, the largest and nearest to the mainland of the Farne Islands. The island is about 16 acres in area and on the western side has precipitous jagged cliffs, but slopes away more gently to the eastern side where the rocks encircle a small white sandy beach, where small boats can land. During the breeding season, terns lay their eggs and hatch their young almost anywhere but still dive furiously at anyone who inadvertently dares to go near them. Puffins squat solemnly in small parties on flat rocks, regularly diving for sand eels while kittiwakes and shags nest perilously and hatch their young on tiny ledges all down the side of the cliff faces. The placid eider ducks make their nests almost anywhere in the tufts of wiry grass; with their trusting nature and apparent lack of fear great care has to be taken not to stand on them as they sit quietly on their eggs. The Farnes are much the same today as they were over 1,300 years ago when a small boat landed, bringing the man who was to reign affectionately over this tiny kingdom and its feathered subjects for ten years.

We are told by Bede that nobody dared to live on the islands because they were already inhabited by 'phantoms and demons'; these, however, were soon driven out by Cuthbert's armoury of faith and holiness, never to return.

Almost as soon as he had landed on Inner Farne, Cuthbert set about building himself somewhere to live. He built two small huts out of rock and soil, roofed with rough timber and straw, one as a living room and the other to serve as an oratory. Around these he built a wall of rough stone and turf to form a small enclosure; the interior was dug several feet deeper than the surrounding ground level. Thus, when the building was done, the height of the wall from floor-level inside the enclosure was twice the height of a man; this was done, Cuthbert said, so that he could restrain his view to concentrate only on higher things.

The outer wall was considered to be a particularly impressive construction by the brethren of Lindisfarne – it contained some enormous stones which Cuthbert had put into position completely unaided. He did ask for assistance with one huge stone and asked four monks to bring their cart from another part of the island to help, but they really struggled and by the time they had got halfway they had damaged the cart, almost injured themselves, and abandoned the attempt. However, on their

Above left: Lindisfarne Church
The early English chancel and altar, St Mary's Church, Lindisfarne.

Above right: St Mary's Church, Lindisfarne
This exhilaratingly beautiful and spiritual place has been a place of pilgrimage for almost 1,400 years.

The Journey by Fenwick Lawson
This sculpture in wood shows the monks of Lindisfarne carrying the coffin of St Cuthbert to his final resting place. It was originally on display in Durham Cathedral but is now kept in St Mary's Church on Holy Island.

next visit the stone had been moved into position in the wall exactly where Cuthbert had wanted it placed. The brethren made frequent visits to Cuthbert in his early days on Inner Farne and a guest house was built for them near to the landing stage – the small, stone fish-house now occupies this spot. Cuthbert would receive and pray with his visitors on the small beach; he would then devoutly wash their feet in warm water and sometimes he was persuaded to remove his own boots and allow the monks to wash his feet too. His mind had become so remote from all bodily considerations he would often wear his boots for months on end – from Easter until the following Maundy Thursday, a year later, when he was obliged to remove them for the ceremonial washing of the feet.

Near the guest house there was a well for use by the visitors, but Cuthbert's dwelling had none and he pointed this out to the monks on one of their visits: 'Beloved brethren, you see that this place can be scarcely inhabited owing to the lack of water and so we will pray to God for His help, and you shall dig down into this rocky ground in the midst of the floor of my dwelling, for God is able to bring forth water from this hard rock if we ask Him.' And so, while Cuthbert knelt and prayed, the monks dug and soon fresh water seeped into the hole. It continued to flow steadily, neither drying up nor overflowing, and that well is still there today, a source of fresh drinking water.

Gradually Cuthbert made the island habitable, although he still needed one or two things. He had planned to build a little chamber to serve as a closet over a narrow cleft in the rocks washed by the sea, and so he asked the monks to bring a piece of timber about 12 feet long with them on their next visit. However, they forgot and it wasn't until after Cuthbert had prayed with them and asked them about the piece of timber that they realised and confessed their forgetfulness. He promptly forgave them and urged them to rest on the island until the following day, adding that God would not forget his needs. The monks stayed in the guest house that night and next morning they found that the night tide had miraculously washed in a piece of timber of the right size and placed it exactly in the required place.

Cuthbert had a good supply of fresh water on the island and his bread was brought over from Lindisfarne but he felt that he should be self-sufficient and so asked for some tools and a supply of seed that he might grow his own wheat. He sowed the seed in spring but no wheat had appeared by the middle of the summer. Disappointed, he said to the brethren:

> It is not suitable to the soil, or perhaps it is the will of God that wheat won't grow here for my benefit. Bring me some barley instead and we will see if that produces a crop. And if God does not permit a harvest from that I would rather return to the monastery than remain here supported by the labours of others.

In spite of being sown late in the season the barley still yielded an excellent crop. As soon as it began to ripen it attracted a flock of hungry birds. Cuthbert approached them and said, 'Why do you attack these crops you have not sown? Is your need greater than mine? If you have God's permission please continue to do what he allows you.

Cuthbert of Farne
The original sculpture of
Cuthbert of Farne was carved
from an elm tree in 1983 by
Durham sculptor Fenwick
Lawson and put on display
in the cloisters of Durham
Cathedral. In 1999, the
Northern Rock Foundation
commissioned it to be cast
in bronze and displayed in
Lindisfarne Priory.

Lindisfarne is a wonderfully atmospheric place; a low, windswept, almost flat tidal island,
punctuated with two defendable crags, on one the castle, the other protecting the priory and the
church, and a small safe harbour.

Otherwise depart and do not injure the possessions of another.' At his words the birds rose as one and flew away and never attacked his barley again.

Cuthbert's relationship towards animals was always kind and happy; in fact the gentle, placid Eider Ducks which live on the Farnes and the Northumberland coast are known to this day as 'Cuddy's Ducks'. There is another story about Cuthbert and two ravens which happened at this time. These two birds had lived on the island for some time and one morning Cuthbert saw them tearing straw from the roof of the guest house to use in building a nest. With a slight movement of the hand Cuthbert signalled them to stop but they ignored him. He became angry, and sternly told them to depart from the island in the name of Jesus Christ and never to return. Bede says, 'They flew dismally away.' However, three days later one of them returned while Cuthbert was working on his crops – it approached him with bowed head, outspread wings and ruffled feathers as if to beg forgiveness. Cuthbert guessed its meaning and quickly forgave it – the bird flew eagerly away to fetch its mate. Soon they both reappeared each carrying a piece of pork fat in their beaks, which they placed at Cuthbert's feet as an offering. This was a valuable commodity in its own right and the writer of Cuthbert's anonymous biography says he was told by 'trustworthy visitors' that for a whole year they greased their boots with this lard.

Cuthbert's withdrawal from active life at the monastery did not mean he was forgotten; his tiny realm had become famous and many people came to visit, not only from Northumbria but also from the remote corners of Britain, all attracted by the fame of his miracles. Inner Farne is only a mile and a half off the coast, where Seahouses now stands. Some would travel from here and others would make the seven-mile journey from Lindisfarne, bringing him their fears, sins and ailments, hoping for consolation; we are told that not one visitor returned from their visit to the hermit still bearing their troubles and sorrows.

The constant stream of visitors and Cuthbert's growing fame greatly impressed the monks of Lindisfarne but he constantly told them that they should not regard him as special because he chose to live alone. He said,

> It is the monastic life that should be admired because brethren are, in all respects, subject to the orders of the abbot and everything they do is governed by his judgement. I know many monks who greatly exceed me, weak as I am, both in purity of heart and in prophetic grace.

He went on to tell them about Boisil, his old prior, who had taught him everything in those early days at Melrose and, indeed, how he had prophesied everything that would happen to him. 'And of all those things which he foretold to me, only one remains unfulfilled and I would hope that it might never come to pass.' He referred, of course, to the office of bishop, to which he dreaded being appointed because it would mean the end of the solitary life that he loved so much.

For about three years Cuthbert lived a life of partial withdrawal, still receiving religious and secular visitors. In 684 his solitude was briefly interrupted by

Hobthrush Isle, just off the island of Lindisfarne, is an ancient place of prayer and contemplation, used by St Cuthbert when he sought solitude for his religious devotions.

Holy Island is linked to the mainland by the modern causeway and the enigmatic pilgrims' causeway, its route marked only by a line of tall stakes.

voyage to Coquet Island for a memorable meeting with Aelfled, the abbess of St Hilda's Monastery at Whitby. She was of royal descent; her father was Oswin, King of Bernicia, and her mother Eanfleda, daughter of Edwin, King of Deira. She held Cuthbert in great esteem before their meeting because she had experienced first-hand the efficiency of his miraculous power. She herself had told Herefrith, Prior of Lindisfarne, from whom, in turn, Bede heard the story. She had almost completely lost the use of her limbs, and was unable to walk, or stand upright, and she could only move around on all fours. While in the grip of this distressing state she desperately prayed, hoping for something belonging to Cuthbert to help her cure. God made her wish known because not long after a messenger arrived from Lindisfarne with a linen girdle which Cuthbert had sent. Full of joy and confidence, she wrapped the girdle around herself, and by the next morning was restored to perfect health.

By her earnest request, the man of God agreed to see her. The meeting was arranged to be on Coquet Island opposite the mouth of the River Coquet, just off the coast near Amble because it was considered a mutually acceptable halfway house. Cuthbert, accompanied by some of the brethren from Lindisfarne, sailed from Farne, and met Aelfled at the large monastery which then existed on the island.

Cuthbert and the royal abbess conversed for a short while until eventually Aelfled made known the real reason for the meeting. Suddenly she fell to her knees before Cuthbert, and begged him to tell her how long King Egfrid, her brother, would live to reign over the kingdom of the Angles. She was gravely concerned because a great crisis in the politics of state seemed to be near at hand. The long struggle between the kings of Bernicia and Mercia had weakened the Northumbrian kingdom, and now the savage Picts were invading it from the north. Egfrid was well-known for his ambitious and restless character and Aelfled was anxious to learn from Cuthbert when the war he was involved in would end, its outcome, and indeed, what was to be the ultimate fate of the brother she loved so much. She further implored Cuthbert, 'I know that from the spirit of prophecy which you possess so abundantly, you can do this, if you wish.' Cuthbert tried to evade her question, but the abbess pressed him, with tears, to tell her the truth. Cuthbert revealed to her that her royal brother would not outlive the year. She exclaimed, 'Who, then, will succeed him, as he has neither children nor brother?'

Cuthbert remained silent for a short time, and then replied, 'Say not that he is without children, for he shall have a successor, whom you may embrace with sisterly affection.'

Aelfled continued, 'But tell me, I beseech you, where is he now?'

Cuthbert replied, 'You see this wide and mighty ocean, with how many islands it abounds. It is easy for God, from one of these, to provide a ruler for the kingdom of the Angles.'

Then Aelfled understood that he spoke of Aldfrid, who was said to be the son of Egfrid's father, and who at that time was living in exile on the Island of Iona. Before the end of their meeting, Aelfled, who knew that her royal brother intended to make Cuthbert a bishop, urged him strongly to accept the office.

The ruins of an ancient chapel and a solitary cross mark the small island just off the coast, near the monastery where Cuthbert made his first retreat and his first move to becoming a hermit.

The Stacks – The Farne Islands

St Cuthbert moved on to Inner Farne to become a hermit in 678, after serving twelve years as Prior of Lindisfarne. He lived on the island for ten years until he was persuaded to take the position of Bishop.

St Cuthbert's Chapel, Inner Farne
Originally there were two
chapels on Inner Farne, but the
one dedicated to St Margaret
has all but disappeared. St
Cuthbert's Chapel was built
in 1370, but by 1840 the roof
had gone and it was falling
into disrepair; it has survived
thanks to restoration work
commissioned by the Venerable
Charles Thorp, Archdeacon of
Durham, who purchased the
Inner Farnes in 1861. The fine
seventeenth-century wooden
stalls were brought here from
Durham Cathedral in 1848. The
stained-glass window is a fine
example of Flemish Glass while
the wooden altar carries the tiny
wooden mouse, trademark of its
maker, 'Mousey Thompson' of
Kilburn, in North Yorkshire.

Eider Duck
Eider Ducks are known locally as Cuddy's Ducks, a reference to their association with St
Cuthbert when he lived on the Farne Islands. Their placid and calm nature allows extremely
close approach, and great care has to be taken not to stand on them during the nesting season.

Remembering the prediction made to him by the dying Boisil at Melrose, Cuthbert said,

> I know that I am not worthy of so high a station; nevertheless, I cannot escape the decrees of God. If it is His will that I should be subjected to such a burden, I believe that He will restore me to freedom shortly after; and perhaps, after not more than two years, send me back to the rest of my beloved solitude. But I command you, in the name of our Lord and Saviour, that you tell this to no one till after my death.

On this Aelfled and Cuthbert parted, and he and the monks returned to Farne.

Cuthbert had never allowed visitors inside his own dwelling but he did leave it to work the land or talk to visitors in the guest house. Later he only saw the monks through his cell window but as time went on he even closed that and only opened it for the sake of a blessing or some other urgent reason.

Such complete withdrawal would not seem unusual for a holy man in those days and his solitude did not upset his equilibrium in any way – he still maintained his appearance and spirit and was never upset unduly by his sins, nor overjoyed when offered loud praises by those who held his way of life in wonder. Proof of Cuthbert's excellent mental condition is proved by the great competence he displayed fulfilling the duties of bishop, which he was finally persuaded to accept in 685, after ten years of hermit life on Inner Farne.

Puffin
Puffins are the iconic bird of the Farne Islands, nesting in large colonies. The genus name loosely translates as 'little brother' – a reference to its black and white plumage being akin to monastic robes.

Grey Seal
The Farnes have a notable colony of about 6,000 grey seals, and several hundred pups are born every year in between September and November. Could it have been these animals that gave rise to the story of demons and phantoms inhabiting the island when Cuthbert first arrived?

Coquet Island
Coquet Island lies about a mile offshore from the fishing port of Amble and was known as *Cocwaedae* in Saxon times, when a monastic foundation was established there. This was where Aelfled, Abbess of Whitby and sister of King Egfrid, had an important meeting with St Cuthbert; she was to try and persuade him to accept the bishopric offered to him by the king. She is reputed to have extracted a reluctant promise; however, it was Eata of Melrose who finally tipped the balance by offering to exchange his new appointment as Bishop of Lindisfarne for the Bishopric of Hexham offered to Cuthbert.

5

CUTHBERT THE BISHOP

While Cuthbert had been living peacefully on Inner Farne, bitter quarrels and intense rivalries had been splitting the Northumbrian church. Wilfrid had been active as Bishop of York since 669, and his great church-building enthusiasm had introduced grand architecture such as had never been previously seen in Northumbria – or indeed, any part of England. Magnificent, dignified churches rose at Ripon and Hexham, built and gracefully adorned by skilful craftsmen brought from continental Europe by the bishop. But Wilfrid's fame and the grandeur of his lifestyle – possibly unintentional – made him a rival to King Egfrid who consequently welcomed a suggestion from Archbishop Theodore of Canterbury that perhaps it might be better if the Northumbrian Diocese was divided into three parts – with a bishop of Lindisfarne or Hexham, another at York and a third at Lindsey in Mercia.

Wilfrid was bitterly opposed to the plan and hastily departed to Rome to complain to the Pope. Meanwhile, three bishops were appointed and already in office when Wilfrid returned with a decision from the Pope, favourable to himself. Egfrid wouldn't accept it and put Wilfrid into prison for a year and thence into exile while the diocese was divided even further by the consecration of a bishop of Lindisfarne as well as a Bishop of Hexham. In the same year Hilda of Whitby died, and in that following, 681, the monastery at Jarrow was founded; it was shortly to become famous as the home of the Venerable Bede, who was now eight years old.

The newly appointed Bishop of Lindisfarne was Cuthbert's friend abbot Eata, but Tunbehrt, Bishop of Hexham, was deposed in 684, or as some historians believe, he left to found a monastery at Gilling; whatever the reason, a vacancy arose. And so, at a Great Synod at which both Archbishop Theodore and King Egfrid were present, Cuthbert was unanimously elected to the bishopric of Hexham and forthwith both messengers and letters were sent to him asking him to accept the position.

In spite of the prophecies made long ago by his little playmate and by his master Boisil, Cuthbert still hoped to avoid this inevitable fate. He prevaricated, demurred and delayed until finally one autumn day a sailing ship landed at the tiny harbour on Inner Farne. A distinguished group of visitors disembarked on to the rocks and picked their way towards Cuthbert's inhospitable cell – the shrill cries of the sea-birds must have alerted him to their arrival because we are told he emerged from his dwelling to greet the party. Before him stood the king of Northumbria and Bishop Trumwine of the Picts, surrounded by many other important ecclesiastics and nobles. They actually knelt before him, urging him to accompany them to the Synod at which Archbishop Theodore was still presiding. The humble hermit knew then that he could no longer disobey the divine decree and, shedding tears, he went with them to the small landing stage and sailed away from his beloved island.

Cuthbert was consecrated the following Easter on 26 March 685. The ceremony was performed at York with much solemnity by the Primate Theodore, assisted by seven bishops, in the presence of the king and an immense concourse of priests. Eata, mindful of Cuthbert's feelings, made a kind concession to him by offering to exchange his own position from Lindisfarne to Hexham so that the hermit wouldn't have to leave the monastery he loved and could carry out his episcopal duties as Bishop of Lindisfarne.

On the day of his consecration, King Egfrid granted Cuthbert a large tract of land within the walls of York and also the village of Crayke, together with an area of 3 miles around it, where he founded a monastery, and which later provided shelter for his body when its bearers were fleeing from the Norsemen. In addition, he granted the ancient Roman city of Lugubalia (now part of Carlisle), along with the adjoining land, a monastery of nuns and a school in which clerics were trained for the service of the Church.

Even though his deeply loved solitude was given up, the new bishop was still able to continue many of the things he had devoutly followed for over thirty years. The author of his anonymous biography tells us that 'he maintained the dignity of a bishop without abandoning the ideal of a monk'.

Cuthbert must have been keenly watched to see if the spiritual balance he had maintained through ten years of isolation was affected by the pressures of his new office. However, he didn't change; he dressed simply and ate frugally, no matter whose company he was in – but most of all he maintained the dignity of his office by the humility and grace that had always been fundamental to his character. Personal holiness was still considered the most necessary qualification for a bishop and Cuthbert didn't neglect his flock. Just as he had always done at Melrose and Lindisfarne, he regularly set out on pastoral visits; now they extended as far as Carlisle and included confirmations and the ordinations of priests.

During Cuthbert's first year of office, King Egfrid's army was ravaging the Pictish kingdom with great ferocity. After destroying two of their main forts, his army was surrounded at Dunnichen, near Forfar. Cuthbert had travelled to Carlisle to await news of the outcome; Egfrid's second wife, Queen Erminburg, was also there, staying at her sister's monastery, awaiting news.

On the Saturday at about 3 o'clock in the afternoon, Cuthbert was being shown around the Roman remains by Waga, the Reeve of the City, in the company of many important citizens and priests. They were admiring the great wall, with its wonderfully constructed fountain, when Cuthbert suddenly appeared unwell. Perplexed, he bowed his head towards the ground and leaned on his staff and, looking Heavenward, he sighed and moaned in a low voice, 'Oh! I believe the war has finished, and judgement has been give against our people in the final battle.'

A nearby priest asked, 'How do you know?'

Cuthbert, unwilling to discuss it further, evasively replied, 'Do you not see how quickly the sky is changed and disturbed? And what mortal man is able to investigate the judgements of God?'

As soon as possible Cuthbert went secretly to the queen and told her to make for the Royal City, Bamburgh, as soon as it was possible to travel because he thought that the king may well have been killed. He explained that he had to dedicate a church the next day but would join her as soon as possible.

On the Sunday, when he had finished his sermon to the brethren of the monastery after the dedication, he began to warn them in veiled terms about being prepared for an impending calamity. The monks took this at the time to be a warning about a return of the plague – there had recently been a widespread scourge in the Carlisle area. But on the Monday, a messenger who had fled the battlefield arrived with the news that King Egfrid had been killed and his army routed at the very time Cuthbert spoke as he stood by the Roman fountain. His bastard brother, Aldfrid, was raised to the throne in succession, but after this resounding defeat, Northumbria finally lost its supremacy north of the Firth of Forth.

The shock of King Egfrid's sudden death and defeat induced his queen, Ermenburg, to return to live in the monastery ruled over by her sister at Carlisle. Once more Cuthbert journeyed to the city, to give her the religious habit, and to ordain some priests, at the request of the brethren of his own monastery. During this visit – the last he paid to the city – which probably took place in the latter part of 686, not long before his death, a memorable and touching meeting took place between the venerable bishop and St Herbert, the hermit of Derwentwater. He is known to us only through his connexion with St Cuthbert, and led a solitary life in a cell on an island at the north-eastern end of the beautiful lake of Derwentwater.

Sadly, there is no record of how he became acquainted with St Cuthbert, but it is possible he may, in earlier life, have been under his spiritual guidance at Melrose or Lindisfarne. In any event, it seems that it was through Cuthbert's advice that he had chosen to pursue the life of a hermit. The two men were united in the bonds of a most intimate spiritual friendship, and it had been their usual custom to meet at least once a year. Hearing that Cuthbert was at Carlisle, Herbert came from his island home to converse with him, 'In the hope of being more and more inflamed by Heavenly desires by his wholesome exhortations.'

Whilst they were mutually inebriating each other with draughts of Heavenly life, Cuthbert said to his friend:

> Bethink you, brother Herbert, of anything you may have need to ask me, and speak to me about it, for after we shall have departed the one from the other, we shall never more meet again in this world, nor see each other with the eyes of the flesh. For I am assured that the time of my dissolution is not far off, and the laying aside of this tabernacle is at hand.

On hearing these words Herbert fell at the feet of Cuthbert, and, shedding abundant tears, said to him,

Crayke

Records suggest that Bishop Cuthbert
was very much admired by Egfrid,
the Saxon king of Northumbria who
bestowed many fine gifts on his church.
Among his donations was the area of
Crayke (Saxon *Creca*) in 685, together
with all the surrounding land within a
circuit of 3 miles. It seems that Crayke
was intended to be a resting place for
the Bishop Cuthbert on his frequent
journeys between Lindisfarne and York.

St Cuthbert's Church, Carlisle

St Cuthbert's Church, Carlisle, stands on
the site of a previous building dedicated
to the saint in 685. It was rebuilt in 870
and again, by the Normans, in 1095.
It was the only church in the city after
Oliver Cromwell closed the cathedral
in 1644. In 1778, the fourth rebuilding
took place, providing the present church
in the Georgian style.

Stained-Glass Windows in St Cuthbert's Church

There are several remarkable stained-glass windows on the east side of the nave of Carlisle church depicting scenes from the life of St Cuthbert. One of these represents his time spent on the Farnes as a hermit, and another illustrates him being shown around the Roman ruins of the city when he had the vision of King Egfrid's defeat and death at the hands of the Picts.

> I beseech you, by the Lord, do not leave me, but bear in mind me, your friend and companion, and beg of the mercy of God that, as we have served Him on earth, so we may pass together to behold His brightness in Heaven; for you know how I have always endeavoured to live by the command of your mouth, and that in whatsoever thing I have offended through ignorance or frailty, that I have striven to correct, at the good pleasure of your will.

The holy bishop bowed his head in prayer for a moment but soon knew his prayer had been heard and said, 'Rise, my brother, and weep not, but rejoice greatly, for the divine mercy has granted what we asked of Him.'

After this revelation, Cuthbert returned to his episcopal see and Herbert to his solitary cell on Derwentwater and subsequent events confirmed both the promises and the truth of the prediction.

After their parting they never saw each other again but later, on the same day and at the same moment on Wednesday, 20 March 687, Cuthbert would die on his bleak rock in the North Sea, and Herbert in his cell on his grassy island on the peaceful and beautiful Derwentwater.

Cuthbert continued his healing miracles throughout his episcopate and we are told of a paralysed youth who was cured by his prayers, a nun whom he anointed with holy oil to cure the pains in her side and head, and of the dying wife of a nobleman returned to health by being sprinkled with water blessed by Cuthbert.

The plague seems to have been particularly rampant during the second half of the seventh century and many villages were almost wiped out by its ravages. But Cuthbert was determined to visit the survivors of an epidemic in any region, no matter how remote, to bring comfort and peace to them with the Gospel.

In one of these villages, after he had been preaching to the pitiful few who had survived, he gently asked his priest, Tydi, 'Is there anyone else still suffering this dreadful plague with whom I may pray and give my blessing?'

The priest pointed to a woman who was weeping for one son already dead of the plague and another held in her arms whose swollen and exhausted body was showing advanced symptoms of the same disease; the bishop approached her and, kissing and blessing the dying child, said to her, 'Please do not weep, your son shall be cured and no more of your family will be taken by this dreadful plague.' We are told that both mother and son lived a great many more years, showing the true word of the prophecy.

Although Cuthbert's ability to heal diseases impressed his contemporaries, it was his prophecies and visions that proved saintliness more than anything else. One such miracle is told in interesting detail by Bede.

It occurred during Cuthbert's last tour of his diocese, after he had decided to give up his pastoral office. He received a message from his friend, Abbess Aelfled, to dedicate a church on her estate. During the meal that was given in his honour he fell into a trance – his limbs relaxed, his eyes took on a fixed stare and his colour changed – and the knife he was holding fell on to the table. His priest, who was serving, leaned towards the abbess and said quietly, 'Ask the bishop what he has seen – there must be a reason why he has dropped his knife and his demeanour changed – he must have had a vision.'

The abbess turned to him immediately saying, 'Please tell us Lord Bishop what you have seen; there must be a reason why you dropped your knife.'

Cuthbert, trying to avoid telling her that he had just undergone an abnormal experience, replied, as if joking, 'Can I eat all day? I must put my knife down sometimes!'

However, Aelfled was not to be put off and he eventually confessed to her that he had seen the vision of a holy man being carried to Heaven by a host of angels. The abbess asked where this had happened and he told her it was from her estate and that she would tell him the name of this man during mass that next day.

Aelfled immediately sent a messenger to her other monastery at Whitby to find out if any of the brethren had died; however, it was reported that the whole community was safe and sound. The next morning, when this messenger was preparing to leave for Hartlepool, he met some of the brethren bringing a dead brother on a cart for burial.

He learned that this godly man had fallen from a tree which he had climbed to get fodder for his sheep and had in fact died at the very time Cuthbert had experienced his vision at Aelfled's table.

The next day, the messenger arrived back and told Aelfled the story and she rushed into the church to tell Cuthbert, who was saying mass and just about to pray for the souls of the departed. Aelfled breathlessly cried out, 'Please my Lord Bishop, pray for our brother Hadwald who died yesterday falling from a tree!' And so Cuthbert's prophecy was fulfilled.

It is perhaps strange that, in view of the fact that Cuthbert was regarded as a woman-hater, his last two visits before he resigned the post of bishop were to women friends. Not long after his visit to Aelfled he stayed at the South Shields Monastery of Virgins where, Bede says, he was magnificently received by the abbess Verca.

It was during a meal in his honour here that he drank water in preference to the beer or wine that was offered; he then passed the cup, unfinished, to his priest, who passed it to a servant. 'May I drink from the bishop's cup?' he asked. 'Yes indeed, why not?' replied the bishop – the servant drank and found that the water had taken on the flavour of good wine.

Cuthbert's friendly simplicity and lack of pomposity endeared him to all who met him. He had laboured as Bishop of Lindisfarne for only two years when he realised that his earthly life was drawing to an end. He was only fifty-one years old, but it was probably his earlier austerities that had seriously weakened his physical strength, even though his mental abilities were left unimpaired. And so it was with considerable relief and thankfulness that he resigned his office just after Christmas 686. He rowed for the last time across the 7 miles of sea that separated Lindisfarne from his beloved island retreat.

The little boat stood ready at the small landing stage on Lindisfarne with a group of monks standing sadly to say goodbye. One of the older monks asked Cuthbert, 'Tell us, Lord Bishop, when may we hope for your return?'

And Cuthbert, who knew the truth, replied simply to the question, 'When you bring my body back here.'

Cuthbert didn't resume his former life of strict isolation when he returned to Inner Farne, but made it a practice to come out of his dwelling regularly to meet and talk with those brethren who came to visit.

Bede was greatly impressed by the story of the uncooked goose, which illustrated the virtue of obedience. One day, after Cuthbert had finished preaching to a group of visiting monks, he was about to return to his dwelling when he pointed to a goose hanging on the wall of the guest house and told them to cook and eat it before they set out on their journey home. Cuthbert blessed the monks and left. The monks didn't cook the goose, as they had brought sufficient food with them, and so they ate this before they prepared to leave. However, when they came out on to the small beach they found that a huge storm had suddenly blown in and they were unable to set sail. For six days this fierce storm raged and prevented them from leaving – they went to complain about it to Cuthbert, who said they must be patient. And on the seventh day he went down to the guest house to have a word with them and when he went in he immediately saw the goose still hanging on the wall. He pointed this out to them in good humour, gently chiding them for disobedience saying, 'Does the goose hang there still uneaten? Why then does the sea not let you leave? Quickly, dress the goose and put it in the pot so that the sea may become calm and let you leave.'

Left: St Cuthbert Window, Tynemouth Priory
After the noonday rest, which was usually
observed by all religious communities,
Cuthbert felt thirsty and requested a goblet of
water to drink. He made the sign of the cross
over it, as was his custom, and having drunk a
small quantity, handed the goblet back to the
priest who had brought it to him. When he was
passed the cup he raised it to his lips, and, to
his astonishment, the water had taken on the
flavour of wine.

This miracle was related to Bede by one of the
priests of the church, who afterwards lived and
died in the same monastery as Bede, in Jarrow.

Below: Tynemouth Priory
Shortly before he died, Cuthbert visited this
monastery at Tynemouth, which was ruled over
by Verca, a Northumbrian abbess of high birth.
Cuthbert was received with great veneration by
the abbess and her sisters. During his visit Verca
presented him with a linen shroud, which he
kept for his body to be bound in after death.

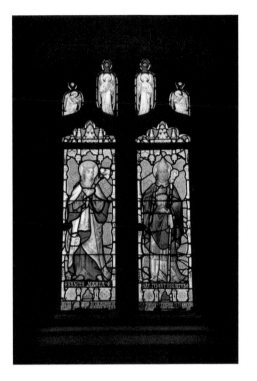

No sooner had the goose started to boil in the pot than the waves subsided and the wind dropped. By the time the bird was eaten the monks had no difficulty in launching their boat to set sail for home, full of joy and shame.

Cuthbert only enjoyed two months of recovered peace and solitude on his little island before he was attacked by the illness that was to cause his death.

He first fell sick on a Wednesday and remained seriously ill for three weeks. Herefrith, who was Abbot of Lindisfarne at the time, was able to give Bede a personal account of Cuthbert's last days because, together with three other monks, he was staying on Inner Farne when Cuthbert took ill.

On the Wednesday morning, Herefrith approached Cuthbert's little dwelling and signalled his presence, wishing to receive the usual blessing and exhortation; but Cuthbert struggled to the window and feebly greeted the abbot.

'What is wrong my Lord Bishop?' asked Herefrith, 'Has your old illness attacked you during the night?' – referring to an old complaint which still troubled Cuthbert periodically after he had suffered from the plague at Melrose. Cuthbert merely agreed and Herefrith, without further questions, asked for a blessing before returning to Lindisfarne. However, he was somewhat taken aback by Cuthbert's sharp reply, 'Yes, board your vessel and return home in safety. And when God has taken my spirit bury me in this dwelling, near my oratory, on the south side.' Cuthbert went on to give further instructions about his burial which, he said, was to be in a coffin hidden under the turf on the north side of his oratory. In this coffin they would find a fine cloth given to him by the abbess Verca, which he had kept for wrapping his dead body.

Herefrith said, 'Father, since you are so seriously ill please allow some of the brethren to stay here and care for you.'

But Cuthbert, refusing, said, 'Go now and return at the proper time.'

Herefrith then asked when that would be and Cuthbert replied, 'When God desires it and when He Himself directs you.'

On his arrival back on Lindisfarne, Herefrith immediately summoned all the brethren into the church and ordered them to offer unceasing prayer for their beloved bishop.

Herefrith waited five days for a raging storm to abate so that he could return to Inner Farne. At last he and a little group of monks were able to cross to the island and they hurried to the rough little guest house where they found Cuthbert, sadly wasted, sitting as if he was waiting for them. Herefrith's companions were urgently needed on Lindisfarne and so sailed straight back, but the abbot stayed with Cuthbert and began the necessary treatments; he warmed water and bathed a festering ulcer on Cuthbert's foot and he warmed some wine and persuaded Cuthbert to drink it; he could see he was suffering from a combination of lack of food and great pain. After his ministrations, Herefrith sat down on the bed next to Cuthbert, who told him that he had been unable to move from this bed for the last five days and nights. Herefrith was amazed and asked Cuthbert how he had managed without food for all this time. Cuthbert drew back the cover and revealed five onions. 'This was my food – whenever my throat was dry and burning I refreshed and cooled myself by tasting these onions.' However, it looked as though only part of one had been eaten.

He continued, 'While I have lived on this island my enemies have never persecuted me as much as they have in these last five days.' Herefrith didn't like to ask which temptations he meant, but merely asked if some of the brethren could remain on the island to wait on him. Cuthbert agreed and among the little group were Beda, who had been used to serving the bishop personally, and Walhstod, who was a brother of exceptional piety but had suffered with dysentery for a long time, which the doctors had been unable to cure.

Herefrith returned to Lindisfarne and told the monks about Cuthbert's desire to be buried on his own island. They all agreed, however, that it would be easier to give his body the honour it deserved if they were allowed to bring it across and bury it in the church on Lindisfarne. The feeling about this was so strong that the abbot and the others put it to Cuthbert again. Cuthbert replied, 'It was my desire that my body should rest here where I have, to some small degree, fought my battle for the Lord.' He also added that it was not just in his interest to have a quiet interment on Inner Farne, as he foresaw that all sorts of fugitives and wicked men would probably seek sanctuary near his body, because of the many stories that had 'gone abroad' about him. This meant the monks would have to intercede with worldly powers on behalf of such people and this would cause them great inconvenience. The monks refused to accept this argument and protested that it would be a pleasure to have this responsibility. At last Cuthbert wearily agreed but asked that he be buried in the church so that while the monks themselves may have access to the tomb at least they would have the power to exclude others if it became necessary.

We are told that, at about nine o'clock on a Wednesday morning, Cuthbert realised his end was near and commanded his attendant monks to carry him back from the guest house to his own tiny house. The monks stopped at the door and sought his permission for one of them to enter with him – Cuthbert chose the afflicted Walhstod, who remained with him until the middle of the afternoon, when he emerged and told Herefrith that Cuthbert requested his company. He also brought the joyful news that he had been cured from his chronic illness the moment he had touched Cuthbert.

Herefrith went into the oratory and found Cuthbert lying opposite the altar. In spite of his feeble condition and difficulty of speech, Cuthbert had a last earnest message for the brethren. With frequent pauses to regain his strength Cuthbert advised that they:

> Should always keep peace and divine charity among themselves; be unanimous in their counsels; be hospitable, kind and humble; keep the monastic rule he had taught them; and observe the catholic statutes of the fathers. He also said that if the monks were forced to choose between two evils he would rather see them lift his bones from the tomb and leave this place and carry them to wherever God sees fit to let them rest than see them in any way submit to evil and place their necks under the yoke of schismatics.

This was a significant statement, and possibly Cuthbert had seen a vision of the violent marauding Vikings who would savagely attack Northumbria a hundred years later;

a group of monks, generations later, would heed his prophetic advice to lift his bones and wander with the treasured burden for eight long years.

Cuthbert lasted, without much further suffering, for another day and another night, at the end of which he received communion from the faithful Herefrith. And then, as he slowly raised his eyes and hands to Heaven in an act of praise, his spirit left the sea-guarded rock that had been his beloved home for ten years.

Brethren were waiting outside the oratory for news, and when Herefrith emerged he found them singing the fifty-ninth psalm. Immediately, one of the monks gave the agreed signal – he lit two torches and climbed to a high point where a monk watching from Lindisfarne, 7 miles away, could see. This watching monk ran into the monastery church to tell the news to the assembled brethren, who also happened to be singing the fifty-ninth psalm, 'Oh God thou hast cast us off and broken us down.' Bede considers this a prophetic coincidence in view of the severe difficulties that were to fall on the Northumbrian Church.

The bishop's body was washed, his head wrapped in a cloth, and the unconsecrated host was placed on his chest. He was dressed in his priestly vestments, with his shoes placed on his feet, ready to meet his Lord. His shroud was waxed to keep out the air and his body placed in a small boat. The body was met at Lindisfarne by a large company of monks and choristers and placed in a stone coffin, under the floor of the church and to the right side of the altar. He was buried on the day of his death, 20 March 687, and this date was thereafter kept as his festival.

6

CUTHBERT THE SAINT

Cuthbert is what is termed as a pre-Congregational saint – he was proclaimed a saint by popular acclamation before an official process for canonisation was instituted by the Catholic Church in the twelfth century. There are stories of several healing miracles taking place soon after Cuthbert's death; the insane son of a man living on Lindisfarne was cured, even though a priest who was skilled in exorcising demons – using the relics of holy martyrs kept in the monastery – had no success. A monk had gone secretly to the place where the water that had been used to wash St Cuthbert's body had been poured away. He had taken a particle of earth, mixed it with the water and given it to the demented boy to drink; the boy was cured as soon as he had taken a sip. And Willibrord, a bishop of the Fresians, was cured of many months of painful illness after kneeling at Cuthbert's sepulchre.

Miracles connected with the body or the belongings of a saint were frequent – and indeed, probably expected – but eleven years after Cuthbert's death an astounding event occurred, which both Bede and the anonymous biographer considered to be of outstanding importance.

It was the custom in those days to open the coffins of holy persons between ten and twenty years after their deaths and to reverently wash the bones, wrap them in silk or linen, and place them in a chest in the interior of the church, where they might become an object of veneration. We are told that, eleven years after the death of Cuthbert, the monks of Lindisfarne sought permission from Bishop Eadberht to raise his relics and place them in a light wooden chest above the floor of the church that they might be worthily venerated. Eadberht readily agreed but stipulated that the ceremony should be performed on 20 March, the anniversary of the saint's death.

The bishop was not present himself when the coffin was open because he was traditionally spending Lent on St Cuthbert's isle, just off the coast near the monastery. He was amazed when some of the monks burst in, full of excitement and terror, to disturb his retreat. They hurriedly explained that when they had opened the stone coffin they had not found bones, as they had expected, but the intact body of the saint lying as if he were asleep. His skin was soft and pliable, his joints flexible, and his clothes were wonderfully fresh and bright; they had brought an outer garment with them so that the bishop could see for himself. Eadberht received the garment with great delight and told the monks to replace it with a new one; and before the body was placed into a new wooden coffin his shoes were replaced by better ones and the head

St Cuthbert's Cave, Northumberland

To the north-east of Wooler, near the tiny hamlet of Holburn Grange, is a natural stone cave set into the Kyloe Hills. This is St Cuthbert's Cave, traditionally thought to have been one of the places where the saint's body rested on its epic journey from Lindisfarne to Durham.

St Cuthbert's Church, Norham
St Cuthbert's Church, Norham, was once affectionately described as being 'half as old as time'. This is not far from the truth because Norham's links with Christianity reach back beyond the time when the first church was established. In 635, when Aidan was called to the great kingdom of Northumbria by King Oswald, he is said to have crossed the Tweed by the old ford here on his way to Lindisfarne.

cloth unwrapped and changed for a new one. Bede would have been about twenty-five years old at the time of this extraordinary event and no doubt heard many first-hand accounts of the miracle from the monks who witnessed the phenomenon.

It was this wonder that established St Cuthbert's fame as the greatest of all the northern saints and the most fitting to become the patron saint of the Church in Northumbria. There had been outstanding holy men in this church already, but the most famous of them – Aidan, Boisil and Colman – had all lived their lives as Celtic Christians and were not really acceptable to those who now followed the Roman tradition. Cuthbert, however, could be honoured by both factions – he was brought up as a Celtic Christian and originally followed their devotions but he had accepted the Roman ways with great obedience and helped persuade his brethren to do likewise.

The fame of this simple hermit of Farne was already widespread, but the wonderful event of his body not suffering decay gave it fresh impetus and the number of pilgrims visiting his simple shrine was steadily growing when, just over a hundred years after the event, a dreadful disaster struck Holy Island, as Cuthbert's retreat was now known.

In 793, an army of marauding Vikings landed in Northumbria. Churches were plundered and Lindisfarne was robbed of most of its treasures; those brethren who escaped death fled inland, and the few who crept back found that, to their joy, the shrine of St Cuthbert had not been damaged. The monastery gradually resumed normal life and this continued in comparative quiet for eighty years. Then a second, more bloody and fierce invasion began – perhaps best described by Simeon of Durham.

> The pagans from the Northern regions came with a fleet of ships to Britain like stinging hornets, and spreading on all sides like dreadful wolves they robbed, tore and slaughtered, not only beasts of burden and sheep and oxen, but also even priests and deacons and companies of monks and nuns. And they came to the church of Lindisfarne and laid everything waste with grievous plundering, trampled the Holy Places with polluted feet, dug up the altars and seized all the treasures of the Holy Church. They killed some of the brothers, they took some of them away in fetters, many they drove out naked and loaded with insults and some they drowned in the sea ...

Fortunately the abbot and the bishop had been forewarned of the Vikings approaching Lindisfarne and, obeying Cuthbert's dying instructions, ordered a small party of monks to lift the honoured body from its resting place and leave the island. Other important treasures were also placed in the wooden coffin; the head of King Oswald, the bones of Aidan and the bones of Eata of Melrose. They also took their treasured copy of the four beautifully illuminated Gospels written in St Cuthbert's honour by his successor Bishop Eadfrid. The sorrowful procession left for the mainland to wander for seven difficult and uncertain years among ruined monasteries and churches on both sides of the border.

Throughout this period of privation and danger the coffin of the saint was carefully protected. No outsider was allowed to touch the bier on which it was carried by seven carefully chosen men – this was such a great honour that their descendants boasted of their connections with these honoured servants over many generations. It is thought

Left: St Cuthbert's Church, Norham
The dedication to St Cuthbert serves as a reminder of the story of how the monks of Lindisfarne fled the island with the body of St Cuthbert and its associated treasures in the face of violent, vicious and terrifying raids by the cruel Norsemen. They made for the comparative safety of Norham, although they did not stay long and soon left on their strange succession of wanderings that would eventually take them all over Cumbria, southern Scotland, North Yorkshire and Northumberland before finding a resting place for their saint's body in Durham.

Opposite above: St Cuthbert's Church, Elsdon
The attractive St Cuthbert's Church stands on Elsdon village green and takes its dedication from the fact that this is reputed to be one of the places where the saint's body rested during its journey from Lindisfarne to Durham.

that one of their descendants was the master-mason who built the beautiful St Laurence Church at Pittington, near Durham, hence the wall paintings of two scenes from the saint's life, which are treasures of this wonderful building.

Wherever the company went their precious burden attracted great respect and affection and indeed many gifts poured in – money, garments, cloths of finest silk and wool, magnificent fleeces, and donations of food from poorer folk. They stopped only in secret and holy places that would offer temporary safety from the Norse raiders. Irksome as this long wandering with the body must have been to those who carried it all that weary way, it must have greatly strengthened the already powerful influence of St Cuthbert; churches dedicated to him have been established in the places where his body is reputed to have stayed for a short while or rested overnight.

For seven long years and more, the pillaging Vikings roamed the whole country, spreading ruin, destruction and desolation; Simeon of Durham said, 'Everywhere the monasteries and churches were burnt, the servants and hand-maidens of Christ subjected to every indignity and insult – fire and sword were carried from the eastern sea to the western.'

The bishop, with those who accompanied Cuthbert's coffin, couldn't find the safety they searched for anywhere; they continued going backwards and forwards,

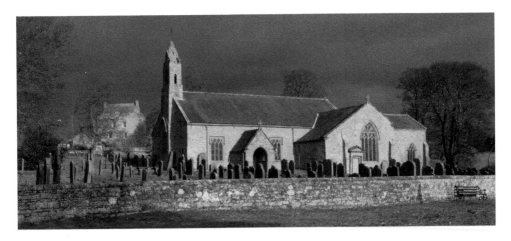

Above left and right: St Cuthbert's Church, Beltingham

St Cuthbert's Church in Beltingham enjoys a beautiful, peaceful setting above the ravine of the Beltingham Burn to one side and close to the South Tyne on the other. This is believed to have been one of the places where St Cuthbert preached during his visits to the more remote parts of Saxon Northumberland. It is thought that this was also one of the places where his body rested in safety when the monks were fleeing the Norse invaders. Indeed, this deep connection with the saint is remembered in a beautiful recent stained-glass window to the right of the altar, illustrating significant events in his life. The piece is the work of Welsh artist Leonard Evetts (1909–97) and is dedicated to Douglas Smith OBE JP, churchwarden and benefactor of the parish.

St Cuthbert's Church, Old Haydon
St Cuthbert's Church in Old Haydon stands on a hill to the north of the modern village of Haydon Bridge. It is generally agreed that the bones of St Cuthbert rested here during their epic journey from Lindisfarne, so there must have been a church on this site before 995, around the time the saint was taken to his last resting place in Durham.

St Cuthbert's Well
A grass path leads from the church down steep steps to St Cuthbert's Well, originally a dipping well. The abundant spring of clear pure water is now contained by a picturesque Georgian pant, its ever-flowing spout directing the water down through a metal grill and away to the River Tyne. The water is still used in the church for baptisms. The locals affectionately refer to this little pant as 'Cuddy's Well'.

Opposite, above left: St Cuthbert's Church, Bellingham
St Cuthbert's Church, Bellingham, marks the site of another halt, in this case on its long journey from Lindisfarne to Durham. The first building on the site was probably wood and was replaced by the present Norman church. It is one of the few churches in England with a massive stone roof, dating from the 1600s – the earlier wooden version had been twice burned by marauding Scots.

Opposite, above right: The Bewcastle Cross
The Bewcastle Cross was erected on this site of great religious importance. It dates from around 675 – the time of Benedict Biscop. It is inscribed with runes and enigmatic figures, worn away and damaged over the years. Their meaning is not particularly clear, although it has been suggested it is dedicated to King Alchfrith of Deira, son of Oswi of Northumbria, who ruled from 641–70. The Bewcastle Cross is accepted to be one of the finest examples of an Anglo-Saxon Cross in the whole of Europe.

hither and thither, as they desperately fled before the face of the cruel and relentless barbarians.

Towards the end of the sixth year, the bishop and his companions began to think it was impossible to find a peaceful and permanent place in England for their saint to rest. A terrible famine gripped the land, caused mainly by the ceaseless ravages of the Vikings making it impossible to cultivate the land. It seemed that the only alternative open to them was to abandon Northumbria and seek safety in Ireland. Bishop Eardulph and Eldred the Abbot secretly assembled the oldest and most experienced of their followers, and told them of their plan in confidence. After carefully considering the reasons, they unanimously agreed to undertake the voyage.

A ship was engaged to meet the little band at the mouth of the River Derwent in Cumbria – probably somewhere near the present-day town of Workington. The Body of St Cuthbert was put on board, those who were in on the secret embarked, and the rest of the monks and the laymen who had followed the body from Lindisfarne were left behind in ignorance of what was about to happen. There was great sorrow and sadness expressed by those who were left, according to Simeon of Durham: 'Miserable men that we are; why have we fallen upon such days of sorrow? Thou, our dear father and patron, art like one carried away captive into exile; we, like miserable and imprisoned sheep are consigned to the teeth of ravening wolves.'

The ship resolutely set sail, but almost immediately ran into a violent storm – it wouldn't respond to its rudder, became absolutely unmanageable, and violently tossed about on the tumultuous waves, narrowly escaping total destruction. As it rolled on to

Left: St Cuthbert's Church, Bewcastle
This church was originally built during the reign of Edward I, using stones from the Roman fort. However, it was rebuilt in the 1700s and the dedication was changed to that of St Cuthbert – a reflection of the huge influence held by the powerful cult surrounding the Durham Saint.

Below: St Cuthbert's Church, Salkeld
There has probably been a church in Great Salkeld since 880, when the body of St Cuthbert is said to have rested here during its epic journey from Holy Island to Durham. It was John de Wessington, a gifted scholar and Prior of Durham in the early fifteenth century, who first compiled a list of the places he believed had been visited by the monks bearing Cuthbert's coffin, based mainly on churches dedicated to him. A wonderfully colourful stained-glass window by James Powell & Sons, of Whitefriars, commemorates its dedication to St Cuthbert.

St Cuthbert's Church, Edenhall

Edenhall is traditionally one of the early churches built to mark one of the resting places of the monks who bore St Cuthbert's body during their seven years wandering after the Viking invasion of Northumbria in 875.

Again, this idea is based on the fifteenth-century writings of Prior John de Wessington. Edenhall lies on the traditional route thought to have been followed by the monks. This would seem to justify the claim to an early foundation on or very near the site of the present church.

St Cuthbert's Church, Edenhall The East window is of particular interest in that it still retains the ancient figures depicting St Cuthbert and King Ceolwyn, although the rest of this great perpendicular window is filled with examples of German glass dating from 1834.

Above and below: St Michael's Church, Workington

Workington is thought to stand at the place at the mouth of the River Derwent from which the monks carrying St Cuthbert's coffin unsuccessfully attempted to sail to Ireland. A tasteful modern window and an illustrative panel in the galleries of St Michael's church serve as reminders of St Cuthbert's connection with the area. The St Cuthbert window has a colourful central panel depicting the saint while the left panel has an illustration of monks carrying the coffin of St Cuthbert to the sea. It is thought they possibly stayed at the monastery which was originally on the site of St Michael's Church.

its side at the height of the storm's fury, the copy of the precious Lindisfarne Gospels was washed overboard into the sea.

As soon as the bishop and those who had been keen to leave England regained the safety of the shore, they fell upon their knees weeping with shame and sorrow, praying fervently for forgiveness; those who had been left behind, who had been weeping from grief, now shed tears of joy.

The first thing the bishop did was to organise a search for the book they had lost, and, to his great joy and delight, it was found at Whithorn, on the opposite coast of the Solway, having been washed up on to the sands by the tide. It was well guarded thereafter and eventually taken by the monks to Durham, and finally restored to Lindisfarne, remaining there until the Dissolution.

Following this incident the interest, confidence and enthusiasm of the brethren diminished. As a consequence of the famine which devastated the north country in the wake of continuing Viking incursions, the greater part of the band of followers, tired from several years' travel, suffering from hunger and lack of comforts, left the party. The only ones that remained were the bishop, the abbot, and the seven faithful guardians who had never deserted their post as protectors of the body of the Saint. It was then that it became necessary, owing to the diminished number of followers, to obtain a horse to draw the cart upon which the body was carried.

Another year was spent in their desolate wanderings, and after suffering great hardships from the extensive famine – especially in the wild and dangerous land of

Isle of Whithorn, Galloway
Isle of Whithorn retains the name although it is no longer a true island – harbour improvements carried out in 1790 included the building of a causeway linking island with mainland, on which parts of the village have since been built.

Above and below: Isle of Whithorn, Galloway

It is interesting that this stretch of coastline is the place where it is believed that the Lindisfarne Gospels were washed ashore after being lost overboard during the ill-fated attempt to sail to Ireland with the coffin of St Cuthbert. The story has it that their ship was driven back to the mouth of the River Derwent in Cumbria and an extensive search immediately mounted for the lost Gospels. However, it is just possible that the prevailing winds and rough tides in this part of the Solway drove the sailor monks aground on this coastline during the storm, giving them reason to search this particular part of the coast and the nearby Isle of Whithorn. Obviously they would have needed to continue their journey back to England and could have made their way directly to Kirkcudbright, another one of the saint's resting places.

the Picts, who then occupied the whole of the country north of the estuaries of the Forth and the Clyde – the faithful monks arrived with their treasure at Crayke, in the neighbourhood of York, in the autumn of 882. Crayke was one of the gifts made by King Egfrid to St Cuthbert on the day of his consecration as bishop. He had founded a monastery there and at that time it was occupied by a group of monks who had returned there after the Viking invasions. The abbot received the wanderers with open arms and gave them shelter, and they stayed there for four months.

The Vikings had by this time established themselves in Northumbria but Halfdene, their king, had been forced, through the hatred of his subjects, to leave the kingdom, and the invaders were left without a leader. At this point St Cuthbert appeared to Eadred, the abbot, in a vision and commanded him to single out as their future king one Guthred, son of Viking chieftain Hardicanute. Guthred had been sold as a slave and was living in servitude at Whittingham in Northumberland. The abbot found where this prince was living, paid the price of his ransom and, following the command of St Cuthbert, proclaimed him king on St Oswin's Hill at Tynemouth by placing a

St Ninian's Cave
To further the Christian connection, St Ninian first set foot in Scotland about 3 miles to the west of the Isle of Whithorn, marked by St Ninian's Cave; the site still holds significant interest for Christians, the number of crucifixes and other religious artefacts left behind showing it to be still a popular place of pilgrimage.

bracelet, the emblem of royalty, on his right arm. Simeon tells us that 'by appointing son of a Danish general of fame, and of revered memory amongst his countrymen, the minds of the people were conciliated, and under the influence of the patron saint the old Northumbrians were reconciled to his government'.

Guthred showed St Cuthbert his gratitude by granting his followers lands at Cuncasestre – present-day Chester-le-Street. The monks settled there at the beginning of 883 and built a fine wooden cathedral, to house the body of their saint and other treasures, which was profusely endowed by the king, and became a place of pilgrimage for the whole of Northumbria. Soon afterwards the king gave, in perpetual succession to St Cuthbert, the whole of the land between the Wear and the Tees, and made his church a place to which fugitives could fly in case of need, and where they enjoyed inviolable sanctuary for the space of thirty-seven days. King Alfred, on whom Guthred was gradually becoming dependent, confirmed the gift, and together they bestowed upon the saint other privileges and immunities. St Cuthbert's body rested here for 113 years, and the town was the centre of a vast diocese which extended from the North Sea to the Irish Sea and from the River Tees to the Firth of Forth. During this period the town was the seat of nine Saxon bishops, and the shrine of St Cuthbert was richly endowed with fine gifts from many notable visitors and benefactors. Among these was

St Cuthbert's Churchyard, Kirkcudbright
The name Kirkcudbright comes from 'Kirk of St Cuthbert' (pronounced *kir-koo-bree*) and reflects the town's early importance as an ecclesiastical centre. Its origin dates from the late 800s, when a church dedicated to St Cuthbert was founded here by Northumbrian monks fleeing with the body of their revered saint and other holy relics from the Viking invaders who attacked their monastery on Lindisfarne.

King Athelstan, who, in 937, sought the aid of St Cuthbert for his forthcoming battle with the Scots – he brought many gifts such as chalices, plates, tapestries, curtains, Gospels, four bells and a cross of gold. His half-brother who succeeded him, as King Edmund, gave magnificent robes and two of his own arm bracelets when he visited the shrine. In 995 the religious community anticipated another Norse threat and they set forth yet again, bearing the coffin of St Cuthbert – this time they found sanctuary at Ripon after a comfortable journey in summer. They stayed in Ripon for about four months and when peace once more seemed assured, the huge party, now about 500 strong, began the trek north again, intending to return to their old site.

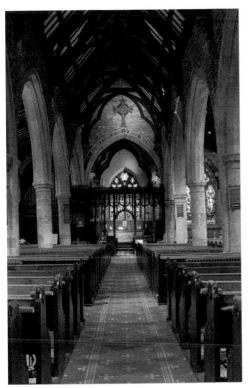

Above left, right and next page: St Mary and St Cuthbert's Church, Chester-le-Street

The old Roman station of Chester-le-Street has a prominent place in the history of County Durham as one of the long-term resting places of St Cuthbert's remains. In 875 the monks of Lindisfarne, under the threat of Norse invaders, fled from their island sanctuary, taking with them the coffin of St Cuthbert. For eight years they wandered the North with their precious burden until they came to Chester-le-Street in 883. They built a large wooden church in which to place the body of their saint and other treasures. St Cuthbert's body rested here for 113 years, and the town was the centre of a diocese extending from the North Sea to the Irish Sea and from the River Tees to the Firth of Forth. During this period, the town was the seat of nine Saxon bishops and the shrine of St Cuthbert was richly endowed with fine gifts from many notable visitors and benefactors. On the north wall of the church are three painted panels relating the history of St Cuthbert and the church – these were done in about 1925 by Archibald Keightley Nicholson, who is better known as a glass-painter or designer of stained-glass windows.

7

ST CUTHBERT OF DURHAM

The party was making good progress on their journey back to Chester-le-Street and had just reached Wrdelau, just to the east of where the city of Durham now stands, when they came to an unscheduled halt. The story goes that the bier on which the coffin was being carried became fixed and no amount of effort could persuade it to move. The saint obviously had no wish to return to Chester-le-Street, but the monks had absolutely no idea where to take him. For three days they fasted and prayed and St Cuthbert appeared in a vision to one of the brethren, Eadmer, and said that they must take his body to the 'Dunholme' – the Hill Island. But where was Dunholme? The monks were deeply distressed because none of them knew. Then, as fortune would have it, one of the brethren overheard two dairymaids discussing the whereabouts of a lost cow – one told the other it had wandered on to the Dunholme. The monks were delighted and, guided by the girl who had lost her cow, they moved the coffin on to this naturally defendable peninsula, formed by a sweeping loop in the River Wear; a place thick with deep woods and thorn bushes except for a little plateau at its centre. Here they set down the coffin and constructed a rough shelter of boughs to protect the precious burden they had carried for so long. They were overjoyed; they had found a final resting place for St Cuthbert.

This story of the Dun Cow is depicted in a relief sculpture on the outside of the north-eastern turret of the Chapel of the Nine Altars of Durham Cathedral – this is a 1799 restoration of the original by George Nicholson, builder of Prebends Bridge. William Hutchinson, the noted Durham historian, wasn't impressed with the restoration and described it as 'restored and finished with much art', claiming it bore little resemblance to the original.

Some historians explain away the story of Dun Cow as a reflection based on an old proverb about the consequential wealth of Durham: 'The Dun Cow's milk makes the Prebends wives go all in silk.' The earliest documentation of the legend dates from the sixteenth century but, whatever the truth, it lends a certain romantic mysticism to the wonderful story of St Cuthbert.

However, soon after their arrival at this chosen spot the monks set about building a permanent shrine worthy of Northumbria's most famous and best-loved saint. In 999 a stone cathedral of considerable size, known as the White Church, was sufficiently advanced in its building to allow St Cuthbert's body to be translated to its shelter on 4 September. The see of the bishop was permanently established at Durham, and

This page: Warden Law and the Dun Cow

Legend has it that the bier carrying St Cuthbert's body stopped at Warden Law and couldn't be moved. After a vision the party was guided to the Dunholme by two dairymaids looking for a lost cow. This was to be the final resting place for their saint. This romantic story is commemorated by a relief panel on the outside of the north wall of the Chapel of the Nine Altars of Durham Cathedral.

On a more prosaic level a stone St Cuthbert's cross sunk into the aptly named Cuthbert Lake commemorates the Cuthbert connection at Sharperley Springs Fisheries at Warden Law, near Seaham.

although this church was not finished until 1017, a stream of pilgrims began to flow steadily. The community of monks did follow a modified, less strict, Benedictine rule but the majority were married men and separate houses were built for the various families around the cathedral.

In the meantime, great events had taken place that would change the destiny of England. Harold, the last Saxon king, had been defeated and slain at Hastings in 1066, and William the Conqueror had been crowned King of England on Christmas Day in Westminster Abbey.

Though the rest of the country at once submitted to the rule of the Normans, the men of Northumbria, of which the patrimony of St Cuthbert was still a part, defied the Conquereor for the first three years of his reign.

To suppress this resistance, William sent Robert Cumin and his earls into the North, with express orders and absolute power to crush it into obedience. Cumin reached Durham, but on the very night of his arrival, the people rose against the invaders and set fire to the house in which he lodged; the Earl and many of his followers were burned alive. Another commander was despatched by the king, but was, as the people of Durham firmly believed, providentially prevented from reaching the bishopric by a thick mist that descended and prevented further advance. At length William himself undertook the expedition, and arrived at York, prepared to lay waste the land with fire and sword. This became known as the Harrying of the North. This campaign was so successful from his point of view that there was not enough of anything left in the North for any entries in his famous Domesday Book – it wasn't until much later, when Prince Bishop Hugh Pudsey compiled the Boldon Book, that there were any records of his assets north of the Tees in County Durham.

When the news of William's approach was known in Durham, Bishop Egelwin, the fourth in succession from Alduhn, called together his clergy at once, and it was decided to take the body of St Cuthbert to Lindisfarne. Their flight was impeded by the severe December frosts, and on the first day they didn't get beyond Jarrow. On the following night they halted at Bedlington, and another day's journey brought them to Tuggall, in the parish of Bamburgh. A chapel dedicated to St Cuthbert was afterwards built at Tuggall, the ruins of which were standing until the end of the nineteenth century.

It was not until the evening of the fourth day after leaving Durham that the fugitives arrived at the coast opposite Holy Island. The night was dark and stormy, and to their dismay the sea was raging with the tide at full height. The protection of the saint did not fail them in their need; to their relief and joy the waters of the sea parted and left them a dry passage across the causeway. It is possible that some kind of partial restoration had taken place at the monastery on Lindisfarne, and it was here that the clergy, with their precious burden, found shelter and safety. They stayed there about three months, and at the beginning of the following Lent in 1070, returned once more to Durham.

The White Church was pulled down after the Norman Conquest and the foundations for the present cathedral were laid by Bishop William of Carileph. He also introduced a community of celibate Benedictine monks from the newly formed communities of Jarrow and Wearmouth to replace the less strict Congregation of St Cuthbert.

This page: St Laurence Church, Pittington

In St Laurence Church, Pittington, is a set of two twelfth-century paintings depicting scenes from the life of St Cuthbert; they can be found in the splays of a window at the western end of the church.

The scene in the left-hand splay of the window depicts Cuthbert at his consecration as bishop – he is the tonsured figure kneeling on the left, having the holy oil poured over his head by Archbishop Theodore. It is thought that the crowned man at the far right of the scene could possibly be King Egfrid of Northumbria, who was also present at the consecration in York.

The painting in the right-hand splay of the window is a unique depiction of St Cuthbert's vision at the table of Abbess Aelfled of Whitby, a close friend whom he visited more than once. Cuthbert, by this time, had become Bishop of Lindisfarne and was invited by Aelfled to visit her at her monastery and share a meal. The painting shows the moment that, when eating at Aelfled's table, he dropped his knife as he experienced a vision of 'the soul of a holy man' being taken to Heaven. The holy man's soul is painted as a small figure lying horizontally across the space, head at the right, legs in the air and one hand extended downwards. Bede's story tells how the vision was confirmed when a messenger brought news that one of Aelfled's servants had fallen to his death from a tree.

This messenger is the young man in a light-brown tunic at the far right of the scene, his hand on the table, speaking to Aelfled, who is wearing a green veil around her head and raising her right hand from the table in shock. A tall man, also in brown, stands behind, and then comes Cuthbert in a red cloak, his left hand gripping the edge of the table as the truth of his vision is confirmed. The table is set with a fish on a dish, a cup for wine or other drink, and bread.

Hanging at the west end of the south aisle are two framed full-scale reproductions of the twelfth-century wall paintings with accompanying text stating that they were done by Mr N. Hamlyn of Bishop Hatfield's Hall, Durham, in around 1888.

In 1104 the new building had made such excellent progress that it was possible to move St Cuthbert's body from its temporary resting place in the cloisters to the famous shrine behind the high altar. The date set for the solemn ceremony was 29 August, but it was decided that first the prior and nine brethren should open the coffin to examine the body.

After deep heart-searching prayer, probably mixed with fear and hesitation, they gathered enough resolution for the daunting task. It is said that they were afraid of God's displeasure at their presumption, but it must also have greatly weighed on their minds that the miracle believed for over four hundred years should be proved to be no longer true. However, they summoned up the courage and opened the coffin to find another one inside, covered with a coarse linen cloth. They realised that this must have been the one that Cuthbert's body was placed in when it was first found incorrupt in 698. This oak coffin was perfectly preserved and once again fear and trepidation seized them before they dared to open this coffin. Eventually, encouraged by the words of a particularly pious monk named Leofwin, they decided to go ahead and moved the coffin from behind the high altar to the middle of the quire where there was more space. On opening this coffin yet another lid was found but this was raised easily by iron rings at its foot and head. They removed the linen cloth inside and found the venerated body lying on its side in perfect condition as if it were asleep.

The monks were overcome, filled with joy and hysteria, by what they had discovered and, weeping, they prostrated themselves and chanted the seven penitential psalms. Then, carefully approaching the opened coffin on hands and knees, they discovered a mass of holy relics beside the body, bones included. They decided to remove these, but this was impossible without first moving the body. One monk was told to lift the head and another the feet and, as they did so, the body bent in the middle because of its flexibility and another monk stepped forward to support the trunk. They then lifted the body and placed it on the chancel floor on some robes and tapestries that had been laid down for the purpose. The bones of other saints were removed but Cuthbert's body was replaced temporarily in its coffin and returned to its original place behind the high altar, as the service of midnight office was now due.

The following night the same brethren carried the coffin into the quire and removed the body to examine its coverings, which were all in perfect condition. The coffin also contained an ivory comb, a pair of scissors, a silver altar, a small plate for consecrated bread, a beautifully worked chalice and a linen cloth for covering the sacramental elements. These were all replaced, along with the head of St Oswald, but the other relics were removed to another part of the church to be preserved for veneration.

The monks noticed that everything in the coffin that had touched the body was preserved intact, but any cloth or wood that had only come into contact with the relics had decayed in the usual course of nature. Indeed, the parts of the coffin supporting these relics had also become damp and discoloured under a layer of decaying dust – a new flooring, fitting exactly over the original but supported on four small feet to keep it away from the infected wood, was fitted and the saint's body was then replaced in the coffin which was covered with a waxed linen cloth.

The next day, a huge congregation of every rank and profession assembled in Durham for the ceremony of the translation of the saint. News had spread quickly that the saint's body had been discovered to be still incorrupt, but among the company of assembled abbots there was one who doubted the truth. Naturally, the monks were indignant that their word should be doubted but the abbot's scepticism fuelled the bitter contention that arose. It was Ralph, the Abbot of Seez, in Normandy, who persuaded the monks that failure to prove this sceptic wrong would only fuel doubt in others and so it would be a good idea to have the incorrupt body examined by a group of responsible persons from outside the community, and indeed, the unbelieving abbot himself should witness such an examination.

The monks agreed but it was decided that the saintly Abbot of Seez, who was eventually to become Archbishop of Canterbury, would be the only one allowed to touch the body of the saint. This he did with determination, bending the neck, working the joints, moving the ears backwards and forwards and raising the shoulders until the body was almost in a sitting position – he proved beyond any doubt that the saint's body was indeed incorrupt.

This was witnessed by many influential men – Richard, abbot of the Monastery of St Albans, Stephen, abbot of St Mary's at York, and Hugh, abbot of St Germain at Ollesby (Selby), Alexander, brother of Edgar, King of Scots, and William, the chaplain of the Bishop of Durham. Also present were about forty other clerics and monks, as well as secular clergy. In addition to these there were many of the brethren of the church, some of whom were assisting the bishop, who at that very time had been consecrating an altar in the cathedral.

A *Te Deum* was triumphantly chanted, the coffin was closed, and the ceremony of the translation at last began. As the sacred and holy body was carried into the open, the vast crowd wept for joy and many of them fell to the ground in adoration, making it almost impossible for the procession to go any further. Outside the eastern end of the cathedral the bishop began to preach a long, wearisome and irrelevant sermon when an unexpected but merciful downpour of rain allowed the monks to quickly pick up the precious coffin and take it back into the church. A solemn mass ended the service and the body was laid to rest in the elaborate shrine prepared for it behind the high altar.

The feretory, in which the shrine of the saint was situated, extended the whole width of the church immediately behind where the reredos, or Neville screen, now stands. It measured 37 feet in length by 23 in breadth. It was first a circular or apsidal shape, just like the apse of the Norman church, but later was changed into a rectangular shape when the transept of the Chapel of the Nine Altars was built in the thirteenth century. Four doorways provided entry to the feretory: two from the sanctuary and two from the aisles; one at the north, and the other at the south end. The shrine stood slightly off-centre in this space, nearer to the altar screen than to the east end of the church. The only account of its original shape is known from what Reginald of Durham tells us.

It was constructed of stone, and was supported by nine stone pillars, adorned by constantly burning lamps. In the year 1372, John, Lord Neville of Raby, expended £200 upon a tomb

The Journey
This is *The Journey* sculpture by Durham sculptor Dr Fenwick Lawson, a version cast in bronze from the wooden original in the church on Lindisfarne. The wooden one represents the beginning of the journey of St Cuthbert's coffin, and the bronze one the end in Durham.

Durham Cathedral
Durham Cathedral, or The Cathedral Church of Christ, Blessed Mary the Virgin and St Cuthbert of Durham, has been described as 'one of the great architectural experiences of Europe'. It is greatly renowned as a masterpiece of Norman or Romanesque architecture. Its building was begun in 1093 and largely completed within forty years. It is the only cathedral in England to retain almost all of its Norman craftsmanship, and one of few to preserve the purity and integrity of its original design.

of marble and alabaster for the shrine of St Cuthbert to rest upon. The work was executed in London, and conveyed by sea to Newcastle at the cost of the donor, and thence to Durham at the expense of the Church.

The omissions of the early historians of the Church have, fortunately, been supplemented by a later writer, in a work titled *A Description of the Ancient Monuments, Rites and Customs of the Monastical Church of Durham.*

This most valuable record is quite unique, and by its help we are able to reproduce almost every feature and every detail of the abbey church, as it was before the accession of Henry VIII. In this work the writer gives the following, a most minute description of the feretory and its shrine.

Next to the Nine Altars was the goodly Monument of St Cuthbert, adjoininge to the Quire and the High Altar on the west end, reachinge towards the Nine Altars on the east, and toward the North and South containinge the breadth of the Quire, in quadrant forme, in the midst of which his sacred shrine was exalted with most curious workmanshipp of fine and costly marble, all limned and guilted with gold; havinge foure seates or places convenient under the shrine for the pilgrims or laymen (lame or sick men), sittinge on their knees to leane and rest on in time of their devout offeringes and fervent prayers to God, and holy St Cuthbert for his miraculous releife and succour, whiche beinge never wantinge, made the shrine to bee one of the most sumptuous monuments in all England; so great were the offerings and jeweles that were bestowed uppon it, and no lesse the miracles that were done by it, even in theise latter days, as is more patent in the History of the Church at large. At the west end of this shrine of St Cuthbert was a little altar adjoined to it for Masses to be said on, onely uppon the great and holy feast of St Cuthberts Day in Lent, at which solemnitie the holy Convent did keepe open household in the Frater House, and did dine altogether on that day and on no day else in the yeare. And at this feast, and certain other festivall dayes, in the time of divine service, they were accustomed to drawe the cover of St Cuthbert's shrine (being of wainscott), where unto was fastened unto every corner of the said cover, to a loope of iron, a stronge cord, which cord was all fest together over the midst over the cover. And a stronge rope was fest unto the loope or bindinge of the said cordes, which run upp and doune in a pully under the vault which was above over St Cuthbert's Feretoire, for the drawingeupp of the cover of the said shrine, and the said rope was fastned to a loope of iron in the north piller of the Feretorie, havinge six silver bells fastned to the said rope, soe as when the cover of the same was drawinge upp the belles did make such a good sound that itt did stirr all the people s harts that was within the Church to repair unto itt, and to make their praiers to God and holy St Cuthbert, and that the behoulders might see the glorrious ornaments thereof. Also the cover had att every corner two ringes made fast, which did runn upp and doune on fower staves of iron, when itt was in drawinge upp, which staves were fast to every corner of the marble that St Cuthbert's coffin did lye upon, which cover was all gilded over, and of eyther syde was painted fower lively images curious to the beholders; and on the east end was painted the picture of our Saviour sittinge on a rainbowe to give judgement, very lively to the behoulders; and on the west end of itt was the picture of our Lady and our Saviour on her knee. And on the top of

Durham Cathedral

Durham Cathedral was built as a place of worship, but also specifically to house the shrine of St Cuthbert, the North's best-loved and most well-known saint, in whose honour pilgrims came to Durham from all over England. It was also the home of a Benedictine monastic community. Described as 'half church and half castle 'gainst the Scot' by Sir Walter Scott, it also served a political and military function by reinforcing the authority of the Prince Bishops of Durham over England's northern border.

the cover from end to end was most fine carved worke, cutt oute with dragons and other beasts, most artifically wrought, and the inside was vernished might be more perspicuous to the behoulders; and at every corner of the cover was a locke to keepe itt close, but att such times as was fitt to shew itt that the beholders might see the glorye and ornaments thereof.

Within the feretory, against the north and south walls, there were almeries, richly decorated, containing a large number of precious relics in costly reliquaries, the gifts of kings and queens and nobles to the saint and the church. Here also hung against the piers and suspended over the shrine and over the nine altars the banners of the Scotch king, captured at the battle of Neville's Cross, together with the splendid banner of Lord Neville until the desecration of the tomb and the suppression of the monastery, when they were all taken down, spoiled and defaced. The sub-prior was appointed Feretrar (or shrine-keeper). It was his office to take charge of the shrine and to keep a record of all receipts and expenses connected with it.

The master of the feretory's chamber was in the dormitory. His office was, when any man of honour or renown was disposed to offer their prayers to God and St Cuthbert, or to offer anything at his shrine, if they requested to have it drawn, or to see it, then the clerk of the feretory (an inferior officer) gave notice to his master, the vice-prior, keeper of the feretory, who brought the keys of the shrine, and gave them to the clerk to open it. His office was to stand by and see it drawn up. It was always drawn up in matins time, when *Te Deum* was being sung, or high mass time, or at evensong, when Magnificat was sung.

The building of the Norman cathedral was not finished until about 1140, and at that time the chancel ended in an apse. Bishop Pudsey planned to build a Lady Chapel in the customary place behind the high altar but the work hadn't progressed very far when cracks and fissures appeared in the walls – probably because the ground to the east of the cathedral falls away sharply to solid rock and the foundations had not been dug deeply enough. By that time, however, the monks of Durham had been convinced that St Cuthbert would not tolerate women close to his shrine and this merely confirmed his dislike of them; consequently the construction was transferred to an area of ground just outside the Great West Door and the Lady, or Galilee Chapel, as it is also known, was built. Inside the cathedral itself, at the west end of the nave, a line of Frosterley marble supposedly marks the point over which no woman may advance.

During the course of the thirteenth century, the apse was pulled down and the Chapel of the Nine Altars was built. From that time the actual fabric of the cathedral remained largely unchanged, however there were still as many projects for the community to complete as the increasing wealth would allow, such as windows, the towers, the beautiful Neville screen with its niches for 107 statues, and the fine monastic buildings, among which the dormitory and kitchen are perhaps the most famous.

Many interesting stories are recorded in connection with the tomb of St Cuthbert. Reginald, the monk of Durham, has carefully recorded the graces, favours, cures and miracles that have taken place at the tomb of the saint from the Conquest up to the reign of Edward I.

Durham Cathedral from the Banks of the River Wear
The western towers date from the twelfth and thirteenth centuries and the 218-foot central tower is the most recent addition, dating from the fifteenth century, with excellent perpendicular Gothic detailing.

Durham Cathedral
The northern aspect of the cathedral faces Palace Green, and here the full majesty of its almost 500-foot length from east to west can be seen. The nave, quire and transepts are all Norman, at the west end is the twelfth-century late Norman Galilee Chapel and at the east end is the thirteenth-century Chapel of the Nine Altars, in the Gothic style.

After the campaign by William the Conqueror to reduce the brave Northumbrians to obedience, he made a successful campaign into Scotland and, on his return southward, took up his quarters for a brief time in Durham; while he was there he laid the foundations of its famous castle. During his stay he naturally became very interested in the history of St Cuthbert, and made enquiries as to whether the body of the Saint really rested in the cathedral or not. In spite of the assertions of all the members of the church, the king didn't really believe the story, and resolved to satisfy himself as to the truth, openly threatening to put the dignitaries of the Church to the sword if the body could not be found.

They were terrified, and prayed to God to help them through the word of his servant Cuthbert. The king said he would inspect the tomb at the Festival of All Saints. The day came and William arrived at the church to carry out his inspection but he was suddenly seized with a violent fever so severe that he rushed from the church, mounted his horse and never drew the bridle until he had crossed the Tees. Tradition says that he fled down the little street called Dun Cow Lane, and crossed the Wear by the King's Ford. The place where he made his sharp exit is now known as 'King's Gate'.

In an original charter preserved in the Treasury of the Dean and Chapter there is an account, given in his own words, of a miraculous cure obtained by the intercession of St Cuthbert, by Thomas, Archbishop of York, in 1090.

> Having been for two years chastised by the scourge of God, and dried up by fever and faintness after an incredible manner, when all physicians held out to us nothing but death, when all the while there was nothing which they could devise to sooth our pains, being warned by a vision, I spent a whole night before the tomb of St Cuthbert, groaning and wailing, and having, from excess of disease and fatigue, fallen into a hasty sleep, there stood before me, in a vision, St Cuthbert himself, who touching with his hand my limbs, one after another, and rapidly passing over the diseased parts of my body, straightway roused me from sleep and restored me to health.

The next event took place in 1346. That was the year of the memorable Battle of Neville's Cross, which was fought in sight of the city of Durham. The night before the battle started, 16 October 1346, John Fosser, then the prior of the abbey, had a vision which commanded him:

> Take the holy corporax cloth, which was within the corporax with which St Cuthbert covered the chalice when he used to say mass; and to put the same holy relique upon a spear point, and next morning to repair to a place on the west of the city, called the Red Hills, and there to remain until the end of the battle.

The monks obeyed the order of their patron and stood all day on the spot where the commemorative roadside cross now stands, praying for the success of the English army, while the archers of St Cuthbert rained arrows down on the Scottish men-at-arms. After the glorious victory gained by the English, the captured banners and pennons of the Scots were carried with great solemnity into the church, and hung above the shrine

Right and below: The Lumiere Festival
A four-night display of light and music held
in the city. Among its highlights was Crown
of Light, a combination of light and music
that saw huge images from the pages of the
Lindisfarne Gospels projected over the north
front of Durham Cathedral.

of St Cuthbert, to whose prayers the English army was indebted for its success. It was shortly after this battle that the prior ordered a most sumptuous banner to be made to hold the corporax cloth of St Cuthbert. It was mounted upon silver rods, and the main pole of silver was surmounted by a silver cross at the top. This banner more than once appeared in the field of battle, always assuring victory to the English. It was carried by the men of the palatinate before Edward I, at Berwick-on-Tweed, and was also carried into the Battle of Flodden in 1513 at the head of Thomas Ruthall, the Bishop of Durham's Army, which was led by Sir William Bulmer.

For the last time, it was raised in 1556; once again at the head of the men-of-arms of the Nevilles and Percies, in the glorious but ill-fated insurrection of the Northumbrians, known as the Pilgrimage of Grace, against the atrocious tyranny of Henry VIII. It was also borne in procession on great festivals, attended by a clerk in surplice and four attendants.

After the Reformation, St Cuthbert's banner was burned by Katherine, the French wife of Dean William Whittingham – the Protestant Dean of Durham who was installed to counter the Catholic inclinations of the North.

Wealth continued to pour in from the stream of pilgrims who visited St Cuthbert's shrine, and the generous gifts of the faithful brought great riches and power to the community. The site was proved to be impregnable many times during several attempted Scottish invasions because the defences of the castle were never stormed. However, great riches and security breed a desire for worldly goods even in a monastery and St Cuthbert, the humble hermit of Farne, would have been amazed if he had seen how the splendour and magnificence of the monastery lifestyle had grown out of his saintliness. Decay slowly set in as cures at the shrine became fewer and gifts became more scarce both in value and number; by the time the monastery was finally dissolved, on 31 December 1539, Durham had already lost its former glory.

Before the actual dissolution, St Cuthbert's coffin was opened for the third time. Royal commissioners were visiting monasteries throughout England and making a thorough examination and valuation of their possessions before finally closing them. In 1537, three of these men arrived in Durham – they were Dr Lee, Dr Henley and Mr Blythman. They found that the tales of the St Cuthbert's wealth had not been exaggerated and they spent some time examining and valuing the precious jewels and ornaments outside of the tomb. Expecting to find more valuables inside the coffin, which they assumed would also contain bones and dust, they broke it open. They were absolutely astonished to find the body of the saint, in his vestments, pure and incorrupt, just as he had been found 400 years previously. The Commissioners ordered the body to be carried into the vestry to await the king's pleasure. This was not forthcoming, and so it was buried by the prior and monks in the ground exactly under the famous shrine, behind the high altar. From that time, the glory of St Cuthbert faded. In 1542, even the cathedral dedication was changed from that of the Blessed Mary the Virgin and St Cuthbert, to the Cathedral Church of Christ and the Blessed Virgin Mary; the plain tomb behind the Neville Screen offered no reminder of the eager pilgrims that had thronged to it except, perhaps, a worn stone where thousands and thousands of travel-worn pilgrims once knelt to pray to him.

The White Church
Some historians believe that part of the original Saxon White Church can be seen, incorporated into the fabric of the Norman cathedral.

Galilee Chapel Wall Painting
The painting of a bishop on the wall, in a recess behind the modern altar in the Galilee Chapel, is thought by some historians to be a representation of St Cuthbert, although he is shown in twelfth-century bishop's vestments. The style of painting is somewhat similar to the Cuthbert paintings in St Laurence Church, Pittington.

The Cloister
On the south side of the building, the cloister would have been the hub of daily life in the cathedral. It was started at about the same time as the main fabric of the cathedral but displays a lot of work from the fifteenth century or later.

In 1827, the grave was opened again, this time in the presence of two prebendaries, the cathedral librarian, and another thirteen observers. Inside the stone grave they found the remains of three wooden coffins, one of which proved to be pieces of the original chest made for the body when it was disinterred in 698. A complete skeleton, swathed in the remains of fine shrouds of either silk or linen, was found in the tomb together with many bones heaped together. The skeleton was carefully removed and it was found that it appeared to have undergone no decomposition in the coffin. There is a legend that says St Cuthbert was removed to a safer resting place at the Dissolution and that the whereabouts of his body is known only to three Benedictine monks – it is said that the body of another monk was placed in the tomb behind the high altar and that this is the skeleton discovered in 1827.

A few treasures had escaped the avarice of the commissioners in 1539; the portable altar, an ivory comb and a magnificent gold pectoral cross encrusted with precious stones, the latter a wonderful example of delicate sixth-century craftsmanship. There were also pieces of silk wrappings, which had probably been placed round the body in 1104, removed along with fragments of the original 698 coffin; these artefacts are all now on display in the cathedral.

Naturally, Durham Cathedral has always been regarded with special affection by the people of Durham and, indeed, St Cuthbert is said to offer special protection to the building and the people of the city during times of great danger. One of the more recent examples occurred during the Second World War on 1 May 1942 at about 2.40 a.m.

The Tomb of the Venerable Bede
Bede was much loved by his community and
exceptionally well thought of by his contemporaries.
He was buried at Jarrow, but around 1020 his body
was removed from Jarrow by Alfred Westoe, the
sacrist of Durham Cathedral, and transferred there,
where it was first placed in a small linen bag in the
same tomb with St Cuthbert. Bishop Pudsey gave
Bede his own shrine in 1370; it was described as a
'costly and magnificent shrine with a silver caskett
gilt with gold'. This shrine was damaged at the
Reformation, but the bones were reburied beneath
the floor of the Galilee Chapel when the present
tomb was erected in 1542.

St Cuthbert Window
The north window at the west end of the nave
represents St Cuthbert; he is dressed as a bishop
and is shown standing on an island in the sea,
surrounded by a large halo of puffins, kittiwakes
and terns – fellow inhabitants during his ten years
on Inner Farne. The window was one of two given
by the Friends of Durham Cathedral.

St Cuthbert Detail in the Transfiguration Window
The Transfiguration Window was dedicated on 25 September 2010. A major work in glass by
Tom Denny, it is full of possible meanings and has detailed figures from the Bible intermingled
with stories from Durham history. St Cuthbert appears on an island in the sea, diligently praying,
surrounded by the sound of the waves.

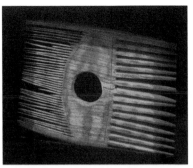

This page: The Relics of St Cuthbert
An excavation by James Raine in 1827 uncovered a
unique collection of objects that have been identified
as the personal belongings of St Cuthbert. The pectoral
cross, the portable altar, and possibly the comb. These,
together with a range of vestments, were preserved
within a series of three coffins, the oldest of which is
thought to be the original that contained the body of
the saint.

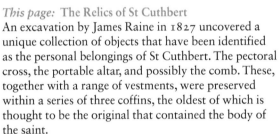

During 1942, Germany launched a series of air attacks against English cities of great historical importance, featured in the Baedeker Guide to Great Britain. These 'Baedeker raids' were carried out as revenge for Royal Air Force bombing attacks against major German cities, including Berlin. The Baedeker raids were conducted by the German Luftwaffe between April and June in 1942. The aim of the raids was to bomb the most historic parts of Britain, thus damaging the British morale. The Germans planned to bomb Norwich, York, Bath, Exeter, Canterbury and Durham – all very historic parts of Britain. They aimed particularly at churches and cathedrals, but their aim was not good enough, and they missed most of them.

Verlag Karl Baedeker was a German author who wrote travel guides, one of which was based upon Britain. It was Baron Gustav Braun von Sturm, a German propagandist, who said, 'We shall go out and bomb every building in Britain marked with three stars in the Baedeker Guide.' The Nazis obviously thought that he knew what he was talking about and consequently based their raids on the more historically cultural but much less strategically important cities.

Gwen Wilkinson, who lived in South Street, which is set high on the riverbank directly opposite the western towers of the Durham Cathedral, was on duty as an air-raid warden when the sirens wailed their eerie sound across the city. Durham was to be the target of one of these 'Baedeker raids'. As Gwen stepped out of the house and walked along the street she was greeted by the unforgettable sight of the cathedral, castle and riverbanks, bathed in beautiful brilliant silver moonlight. She stood admiring the view for what she feared could be the last time – Lord Haw Haw had gloatingly broadcast news of these raids a few nights previously – when a mist began to rise from the river. It soon blotted out the scene, swirling up and around the central and two western towers of the cathedral. A dark cloud blotted out the moon and the whole area was transformed, shrouded in a dark, dense mist. Gwen stood, transfixed; she heard enemy planes approaching. They circled overhead and, unable to locate their target, withdrew. The all-clear sounded and Gwen returned home. As she closed her front door she removed her tin helmet and stood in silence with her head bowed, to thank God for deliverance. She was convinced that St Cuthbert had protected his cathedral, his city and its people.

There are many wonderful stories and legends about this magnificent building and the man in whose honour it was built, but it will always stand as the symbol and the shrine to this humble pioneer of Christianity in the North.

Above left and right: St Cuthbert's Feretory

St Cuthbert is buried in his feretory under a simple marble slab bearing the inscription *Cuthbertus*; however, his shrine was once described as one of the most sumptuous monuments in all England. Its original ornate appearance was said to be decorated with many fine jewels – any one of which would have been worth a king's ransom. The base of the shrine was made of expensive gilded green marble. In the base were four seats, where pilgrims – especially the sick and lame – could kneel to receive the blessings of God and St Cuthbert. It was covered with a richly embroidered cloth, which was raised on special occasions to expose the lavishly decorated shrine itself. The shrine's gilt cover depicted Christ on a rainbow on one side and Christ as a baby being carried by Mary on the other. At the edges of the cloth were six silver bells, which tingled when the cover was lifted, drawing the attention of pilgrims within the cathedral. The current cover of the shrine, a twentieth-century canopy by renowned architect Sir Ninian Comper, is a representation of an idea inspired by the description of the sixteenth-century cover. Cuthbert's relics were placed in their present position in 1104 and Durham soon became one of the most important and wealthiest pilgrimage destinations in England.

8

THE CULT OF ST CUTHBERT

Cuthbert was highly regarded during the time he was a hermit on Inner Farne, prior at Melrose and bishop to the religious community on Lindisfarne – but after his death he became one of the foremost saints of medieval Europe. His importance was demonstrated both by the huge number of pilgrims attracted to his shrine and by the numerous gifts bestowed on him by pilgrims and royalty alike; their generosity made his community one of the most powerful and wealthy in the whole of England. In fact, Cuthbert was considered to be the most popular saint in England, until the death of Thomas Becket in 1170. Towards the end of the eleventh century, his feast days were celebrated in many monasteries in England and, indeed, throughout Europe. His popularity in Europe is apparent from the number of copies of his biography, carefully scribed by continental monks so that their communities should have their own copy. His name also appears frequently in many European liturgical books featuring readings on the lives of the saints. All over England churches have been dedicated to him and to this day his shrine in Durham Cathedral and his beloved island of Lindisfarne have many pilgrims and visitors.

Cuthbert became the object of even more attention and affection after his death and consequently became the focus of one of the most famous and popular cults, right through to the Middle Ages. It was during the eleven years after his death, up to the first exhumation of his body, that the Lindisfarne Gospels were written and illustrated – this volume, with its beautiful script and wonderfully intricate and glorious full-page illuminations, was written in his honour and is regarded as one of the great masterpieces of manuscript illustration. A short passage introducing the manuscript reads, 'Eadfrith, Bishop of Lindisfarne Church, originally wrote this book for God and for St Cuthbert.'

Eleven years after his death, when his body was found to be incorrupt, almost immediately three biographies were written, one by the anonymous Lindisfarne monk and the other two by Bede; one a metrical version and the other in prose. We are told that, although throughout Cuthbert's life he had chosen to follow a path of simplicity and seclusion from the world, his cult was marked by opulence and splendour. In death he was honoured like a great king; his shrine was magnificent, he was wrapped in a beautiful and precious cloth given to him by the abbess Verca, and his body was clothed in fine garments, including a fine white dalmatic, a silk chasuble, and a gold-embroidered alb. A gold and garnet pectoral cross, now on display in Durham Cathedral, complemented the attire. Finally, his body and all the treasures were placed in an elaborate wooden coffin which was adorned with carved images of Christ and the four evangelists' symbols, the archangels Gabriel and Michael and the Virgin and Child together with the twelve apostles and further archangels.

By 995, the community of monks, with their precious burden of St Cuthbert, had moved to their home on what was to be the site of Durham Cathedral and thus began the long association with Cuthbert. In 1083, the monastic community in Durham was established by Prince Bishop William Carileph and the building of the magnificent cathedral was started.

The cult of St Cuthbert was not only extremely important for Durham and its monastic community but also for the whole kingdom of Northumbria in general. It generated an enormous amount of cultural material, such as architecture, books, metalwork, and sculpture. It also, of course, provided the people of Northumbria with a saint who would help, protect and comfort them. But Cuthbert was much more than just a symbol – a lot of land was given to the community of monks who had Cuthbert as their patron – these lands were known as 'The Patrimony of St Cuthbert' and by the end of the eleventh century, those who lived on this land became known as 'Haliwerfolc' or 'people of the Saint' – this forged a great sense of identity among the people and their land became firmly integrated into the whole idea of St Cuthbert.

Above left and right: Replica Banner of St Cuthbert
St Cuthbert's Banner was first mentioned in 1097 when it was carried into battle by Edgar Canmore's army in his bid to retake the Scottish throne from his uncle. Over the next 200 years, the banner was carried into numerous battles against the Scots, and also by the northern rebels during the Pilgrimage of Grace, in protest against the Dissolution of the Monasteries by Henry VIII. Unfortunately, the banner was burned by the puritan wife of Dean Whittingham during the reign of Elizabeth I. It could have been lost forever but a detailed description survived in the *Rites of Durham* and the Northumbrian Association embarked on a four-year project using the considerable skills of local craftspeople to painstakingly recreate this highly significant and important artefact. It was brought home to Durham Cathedral on St Cuthbert's Day, 2012, where it was welcomed by the Bishop of Jarrow the Right Reverend Mark Bryant, and the Dean of Durham, the Very Reverend Michael Sadgrove.

During the eleventh and twelfth centuries, the interest in saints' relics and pilgrimages had reached its peak. The great distance travelled, the suffering, danger and hardship of the pilgrimage to reach the magnificent spectacle of a shrine, richly decorated with gold and jewels, and experiencing the healing powers of the saint – this was all absolutely irresistible. It provided a focus for people of all social classes. Simeon of Durham writes about the shrine that 'men of all ranks, ages and professions, the secular and the spiritual, all hastened to be present'.

The cult of St Cuthbert was thriving towards the end of the twelfth century, but the emerging cult of Thomas Becket, based in Canterbury, challenged the importance and popularity of Durham as a centre for pilgrimage. The murder of Becket, in Canterbury Cathedral, by a group of armed knights, possibly driven by the anger of King Henry II, caused outrage and deep emotion in the minds of people throughout Europe; Thomas Becket rapidly became the focus of the most important cult in England.

In response it was Bishop Hugh du Puiset who attempted to reinvigorate the cult of St Cuthbert – he added the extended feretory and the Chapel of the Nine Altars and the elegant Galilee Chapel at the west end of Durham Cathedral. He also rebuilt Durham Castle, built a bridge to replace the existing ford over the river, built a hospital, and commissioned many elaborate and richly decorated artefacts for the cathedral. Puiset had the walls of his magnificent Galilee Chapel covered with paintings, including those of what were believed to be Cuthbert and King Oswald of Northumbria. These paintings have caused divided opinion – many historians believe it is Cuthbert that is depicted, although there have been theories that it actually represents Bishop Puiset. Regardless, it is reasonable to assume that since he probably commissioned these paintings they possibly reflect some of his interests of interpretation. The painting shows a twelfth-century bishop and appears remarkably similar to how Puiset would have looked in his vestments. In the interests of correctness they are now referred to as a king and a bishop. Interestingly, Cuthbert is also depicted as a bishop in wall paintings at St Laurence Church, Pittington, just a few miles to the east of the cathedral.

Another important man who attempted to revive the Cuthbert cult in the twelfth century was Reginald of Durham, who was probably the greatest author of saints' lives since Bede. He also wrote of the lives of Godric of Finchale, St Oswald, and Ebba of Coldingham. Reginald's book is in two sections: the first 111 chapters were written before January 1167, and the rest were finished by late 1174. The earlier miracles recorded by Reginald occurred on Lindisfarne or the Farne Islands while most of the later miracles take place in and around Durham Cathedral.

Some historians believe that, since Becket was martyred in 1170, it is possible that the second set of stories were added in response to the increasing popularity of the shrine in Canterbury.

However, St Cuthbert survived this crisis in the twelfth century well; perhaps not as a national saint, but certainly as a saint whose roots and home are firmly established in the North of England.

Today over 600,000 visitors a year visit the shrine of this well-loved and highly respected saint, his shrine housed in what is arguably the most beautiful religious building in the world – Durham is one of only two cathedrals in Great Britain inscribed as a World Heritage Site.